Stereotypes, Cognition and Culture

What are stereotypes and why do we use them? Are all stereotypes bad? Can we stop people from using them? Questions such as these have fascinated psychologists for many years. Perry R. Hinton provides an accessible introduction to this key area, giving a critical and concise overview of the influential theories and approaches, as well as insights into recent work on the role of language and culture in stereotyping.

Perry R. Hinton is Principal Lecturer in Psychology at the University of Luton. His previous publications include *Psychology of Interpersonal Perception* (1993) and *Statistics Explained* (1995).

Psychology Focus

Series editor: Perry Hinton, University of Luton

The Psychology Focus series provides students with a new focus on key topic areas in psychology. It supports students taking modules in psychology, whether for a psychology degree or a combined programme, and those renewing their qualification in a related discipline. Each short book:

- presents clear, in-depth coverage of a discrete area with many applied examples
- assumes no prior knowledge of psychology
- has been written by an experienced teacher
- has chapter summaries, annotated further reading and a glossary of key terms.

Also available in this series:

Friendship in Childhood and Adolescence
Phil Erwin

Gender and Social Psychology
Vivien Burr

Jobs, Technology and People
Nik Chmiel

Learning and Studying
James Hartley

Personality: A Cognitive Approach
Jo Brunas-Wagstaff

Intelligence and Abilities
Colin Cooper

Stress, Cognition and Health
Tony Cassidy

Types of Thinking
Ian Robertson

Psychobiology of Human Motivation
Hugh Wagner

Psychology and 'Human Nature' (forthcoming)
Peter Ashworth

Stereotypes, Cognition and Culture

■ Perry R. Hinton

First published 2000
by Psychology Press
27 Church Road, Hove, East Sussex
BN3 2FA

Simultaneously published in
the USA and Canada
by Taylor and Francis, Inc.
325 Chestnut Street, Suite 800,
Philadelphia, PA 19016, USA

*Psychology Press is part of the Taylor
& Francis Group*

© 2000 Perry R. Hinton

Typeset in Sabon by
Florence Production Ltd, Stoodleigh,
Devon

Printed and bound in Great Britain by
Biddles Ltd www.biddles.co.uk

*British Library Cataloguing in
Publication Data*
A catalogue record for this book is
available from the British Library

*Library of Congress Cataloging in
Publication Data*
Hinton, Perry R. (Perry Roy), 1954 –
  Stereotypes, cognition, and culture /
  Perry R. Hinton.
    p. cm.—(Psychology focus)
  Includes bibliographical references
  and index
  ISBN 0–415–19865–8
  ISBN 0–415–19866–6 (pbk.)
  1. Stereotype (Psychology)
  2. Cognition and culture.
  I. Title. II. Series.

BF323.S63 H565 2000
303.3′85—dc21   00-020805

ISBN 0–415–19866–6 (pbk)

ISBN 0–415–19865–8 (hbk)

For Anna, Anthony and Emma

Contents

Series preface

The Psychology Focus series provides short, up-to-date accounts of key areas in psychology without assuming the reader's prior knowledge in the subject. Psychology is often a favoured subject area for study, since it is relevant to a wide range of disciplines such as Sociology, Education, Nursing and Business Studies. These relatively inexpensive but focused short texts combine sufficient detail for psychology specialists with sufficient clarity for non-specialists.

The series authors are academics experienced in undergraduate teaching as well as research. Each takes a topic within their area of psychological expertise and presents a short review, highlighting important themes and including both theory and research findings. Each aspect of the topic is clearly explained with supporting glossaries to elucidate technical terms.

The series has been conceived within the context of the increasing modularization which has been developed in higher education over the last decade and fulfils the consequent need for clear, focused, topic-based course material. Instead of following one course of study, students on a modularization programme are often able to choose modules from a wide range of disciplines to complement the modules they are required to study for a specific degree. It can no longer be assumed that students studying a particular module will necessarily have the same background knowledge (or lack of it!) in that subject. But they will need to familiarize themselves with a particular topic rapidly since a single module in a single topic may be only 15 weeks long, with assessments arising during that period. They may have to combine eight or more modules in a single year to obtain a degree at the end of their programme of study.

One possible problem with studying a range of separate modules is that the relevance of a particular topic or the relationship between topics may not always be apparent. In the Psychology Focus series, authors have drawn where possible on practical and applied examples to support the points being made so that readers can see the wider relevance of the topic under study. Also, the study of psychology is usually broken up into separate areas, such as social psychology, developmental psychology and cognitive psychology, to take three examples. Whilst the books in the Psychology Focus series will provide excellent coverage of certain key topics within these 'traditional' areas, the authors have not been constrained in their examples and explanations and may draw on material across the whole field of psychology to help explain the topic under study more fully.

Each text in the series provides the reader with a range of important material on a specific topic. They are suitably comprehensive and give a clear account of the important issues involved. The authors analyse and interpret the material as well as present an up-to-date and detailed review of key work. Recent references are provided along with suggested further reading to allow readers to investigate the topic in more depth. It is hoped, therefore, that after following the informative review of a key topic in a Psychology Focus text, readers will not only have a clear understanding of the issues in question but will be intrigued and challenged to investigate the topic further.

Introduction

Introduction

OFTEN THROUGH OUR OWN experience, or through the media, we learn of people being stereotyped. A young black man who witnesses a crime is treated as though he is a criminal rather than a witness. A middle-aged man applying for a job is not judged on his experience and wisdom but is regarded by the interviewers as 'too old', and they appoint a much less qualified younger person. A woman taking her child to a doctor is treated as a 'fussy mother' and her concerns are dismissed, only later to be proved correct when the child nearly dies. The advice of a young woman chemist is ignored in favour of less informed opinion, and she is treated in a condescending manner by her colleagues who focus on her youth and good looks rather than her first-class knowledge of chemistry. A child is not encouraged in school because the teachers judge him as uninterested and unintelligent, yet when he transfers to another school he blossoms into a high flyer.

It is clear that stereotyping can lead to a person being treated unfairly. Indeed, in the examples above, all of the people suffer from the prejudice that results from the stereotyping. Notice that the people doing the judging may also lose out as a result of their misjudgement. A witness who is treated badly may not choose to help the authorities again. The best candidate is not given the job when the experienced man is ignored due to the irrelevant characteristic of age. It is a doctor's failure to misdiagnose and nearly lose a patient. Ignoring the good advice of the young woman chemist may lead to problems for the company. Finally, the goal of teachers is to help children reach their potential not to restrict it.

In these cases it seems strange that people stereotype at all when the person being judged is unfairly discriminated against and the person making the judgement does not appear to gain any advantage. Not surprisingly we hear people saying in the media that stereotyping is wrong and that we should try to stop it. What if we tell the employers that the best candidate is not being given the job and the advice of the best chemist is being ignored due to judgements based on stereotypes of age rather than more sensible criteria? It certainly would be nice to believe that we only had to point out the errors in judgement and people would stop. However, as we shall see in this book, stereotyping is more complex than that. It is quite possible that, despite what we say, people will continue to believe in the stereotypes they hold.

Another problem is that we are 'people' too. If we need to convince others of the errors of their stereotyping, what about us? Do other people need to convince us of the errors of our judgements? Also, how can we distinguish between a 'sensible' judgement and a stereotypical one? If you are walking home late one night and you see a young man with short hair and boots coming towards you carrying a baseball bat, is it sensible to slip down a side road to avoid him or should you walk on unconcerned (convinced that your judgement of him as a potential violent attacker is simply a stereotype and therefore a misjudgement)? Which is the sensible judgment here? Is there an element of truth in some stereotypes?

The question is: when is our everyday understanding of people a stereotype and when is it not? Take, for example, what we know about ageing. Unfortunately, as we get older we do become physically less able – arthritis and other ailments can affect many people. So it is not a stereotype to see older people as less physically able than younger people. But this is not true for everyone; the effects of ageing are different for different people. There are many physically fit and active older people with mental and physical fitness far outstripping people many years younger. So the first thing we should note is that in reality older people differ in their physical and mental abilities just like any other age group. A stereotype of older people arises when we assume that *all* older people have the characteristics of physical and mental frailty. Perceiving all the members of a particular social group to be the same on certain characteristics appears to be a key feature of stereotyping. Stereotyping ignores the variability within a group of people.

Yet we do encounter examples that indicate the variation in people, such as the 80-year-old running a marathon. How do we deal with this information? Does it dispel the stereotyped view that all older people are frail? Interestingly, as we shall see in the book, counter-evidence is not always going to lead to a change of view. Pointing out evidence to counter a stereotype may not lead to it being abandoned. Surprisingly it may even be taken as support for the stereotyped view. If the runner is seen as 'the exception that proves the rule', then it may simply confirm the stereotype. The fact that an eighty-year-old marathon runner is seen to be noteworthy might lead people to see that as confirming their belief that older people are *usually* frail, with this being the exceptional case. Thus, we need to examine how people make sense of the information they learn about others before we can decide why and how they might change their stereotypical views.

Consider the example of the child failing to learn in school. If asked why this is, the teachers might say it is because the boy is uninterested in learning. They might even say that he is from a particular ethnic group that is seen to be less able than others. This gives us a second insight into stereotypes: they provide *a particular explanation of events*. The boy's failure to learn is located in an assumed characteristic of his personality, or his ethnic group, of lack of interest or ability. Thus, the stereotype places the cause of the boy's failure to learn squarely on his shoulders, not on the teaching style and methods of the teachers or the institutional system of schooling. Stereotypes may not be simply a view of the world that is either right or wrong, but linked into a person's understanding of why people are as they are. Viewing a child as incapable of learning (due to an inferred characteristic in the child) then allows the teachers to avoid seeing themselves as culpable in the child's failure to learn: it is the fault of the child (or his genes), not that of the teachers or the school or the education system. So stereotypes can provide people with explanations they may be happy to accept. Also the explanation may appear to work. The child does fail, apparently confirming the teachers' view of him. Even when the child changes school, it is quite possible that the teachers never find out that the child did well in the new school.

Categorizing people

Much of this book will focus on the view that stereotyping involves judging people as category members rather than individuals. In stereotyping a woman as a *redhead* we are not treating her as an individual called Mary Jones but as a 'typical' redheaded person with the expectations of a fiery temper. Rather than judging Pierre Duchamps on his individual characteristics, by categorizing him as French we may stereotypically view him as cultured, a good cook and a good lover.

In many of our everyday encounters with people we learn very little about them, but what we do learn is often information that can be used to categorize them. We notice the physical features of passers-by, such as the colour of their skin or their age or gender. The clothes people wear and their style of hair are all to be seen. We can use this information to make stereotypical inferences about what they are like. Many occupations, such as police officers and firefighters, wear uniforms to identify themselves. We observe a man wearing a smart suit and carrying a leather briefcase striding into an office block. What sort of a man is he? What occupation does he have? A young woman in jeans and T-shirt passes by with books under her arm. Can we predict her interests or activities?

Much of our social perception 'goes beyond the information given' (Bruner, 1973). We make inferences, we hold assumptions about certain categories of people. An arts student might be disappointed to learn that a blind date is a science student. The arts student is making an assumption about the character and interests of the blind date based on category membership ('science student') rather than any knowledge of the individual person. Furthermore the disappointment is due to the expectation that the person will be stereotypical of the category and hence not someone they will get on with. They may have a great time on the date and the expectations are disconfirmed. But the expectations may be confirmed, particularly if the arts student starts the date with a negative attitude towards the science student. But it might not get to that: the arts student may simply pass on the date.

A lot of the time we are judging other people, both formally, such as in a courtroom, or informally in our everyday lives. Who do we stop in the street to ask the time? Which colleague at work do we trust to get a report done on time? If we view someone as a category member (e.g. a nurse) and evoke the stereotype of the category (e.g. caring) we no longer have an unknown person but now have a range of assumptions and expectations about that person. Much of the study of judging other people has emphasized the view that we see people as members of a particular category of people based on certain characteristics such as age, gender, ethnicity or occupation. The central aspect of this book is analysis of why and how these categorical judgements take place.

What is a stereotype?

There is general agreement within psychology as to the key features of a stereotype. However, there are differences in the explanation of how and why stereotyping takes place. But to start

INTRODUCTION

with a definition: essentially a stereotype has three important
components.

1   A group of people are identified by a specific *characteristic*.
This can be anything from a nationality such as *English*, a
religious belief such as *Jewish*, ethnicity such as *African
American*, gender such as *women*, age such as *teenager*, an
occupation such as *tax inspector*, hair colour such as *redhead*
– in fact any characteristic that has meaning to the people
doing the attribution. So we might identify a group of people
on the characteristic that they are supporters of a specific
football team or owners of a particular make of car, as well
as on more obvious physical attributes, such as age, ethnicity
or gender.
    What this identification does is to separate from an undif-
ferentiated set of people a particular identified group on the
chosen characteristic. By identifying the group on this characteristic we are able to distinguish them from other groups
on this characteristic. In identifying *redheaded people* we are
separating them from people who do not have red hair
(blondes, brunettes). In identifying a group as *English* we
are distinguishing them from other national groups, such as
Greeks and Italians.

2   We then attribute a set of *additional characteristics* to the
group as a whole. Thus redheads are seen as *quick-tempered*
and the English as *tradition-loving*. Notice how these characteristics are usually personality characteristics, but they
need not be. Some stereotypes include physical characteristics, such as *grey-haired* for the elderly or *tall* for
Scandinavians. The important feature of a stereotype is the
attribution of these additional characteristics to all members
of the group. Interestingly, it has not always been seen as
the role of psychology to discover why a particular set of
characteristics is applied to a certain group. Tajfel (1969)
argues that it is for the social historian to determine why,
within a particular culture, certain attributes get assigned to
certain groups. Rather it is the task of psychology to explain
why we stereotype at all.

7

3   Finally, on identifying a person as having the identifying meaningful characteristic (we discover someone is *English*), we then attribute the stereotypical characteristic to them. So we will infer that this English person, like all English people, is tradition-loving.

The psychology of stereotyping

The question why we stereotype has occupied psychologists since the 1920s. It is clear from the definition given above that stereotypes are generalizations and therefore do not reflect the individual differences within a category of people. Why do we make these categorical judgements? Why do we assume that a person has certain characteristics due to their group membership rather than viewing them as an individual? These are questions that have been considered in the research into stereotyping.

Lippmann's view

The study of stereotyping within the social sciences is commonly agreed to have begun with the book *Public Opinion* by Walter Lippmann, published in 1922. In this book Lippmann introduced the concept of a *stereotype* and gave his views on how and why stereotypes are used. Stereotypes are simplified 'pictures in our heads' (Lippmann, 1922, p. 3) of people and events in the world. Lippman argued that our actions are not based on a direct knowledge of the 'real' world because the 'real environment is altogether too big, too complex, and too fleeting for direct acquaintance' (Lippmann, 1922, p. 16). To cope, we construct these 'pictures' of the environment (including the people and events within it), and our actions do not arise from a 'direct and certain knowledge' (p. 25) of these people and events, but are based on the simplified 'pictures'. We act on the basis of what we imagine to be the case, not what is actually the case. Lippmann accepted that these pictures might be 'made' by the person or 'given' by their culture (p. 25). In particular, he emphasized the importance of culture in defining the pictures.

> In the great blooming, buzzing confusion of the outer world we pick out what our culture has already defined for us, and we tend to perceive that which we have picked out in the form stereotyped for us by our culture.
>
> (Lippmann, 1922, p. 81)

Lippmann claimed that the stereotypes we construct are essentially false, criticizing both the process of producing them and their contents. He argued that a key feature of a stereotype is that it 'imposes a certain character on the data of our senses before the data reach the intelligence' (p. 98) and that the actual contents of the stereotype will always be largely incorrect. Furthermore, he argued that stereotypes are both rigid in their definition and resistant to change.

The importance of describing Lippmann's views here is that it brings out the key ideas that have been debated in the subsequent decades, and that have been the focus of stereotype research for the last twenty-five years. First, we have the view that stereotypes arise from the limitations of human *cognitive processes*: perception and 'knowledge' are arrived at through the process of constructing simplified 'pictures' of the world. Second, the contents of stereotypes are provided by the *culture* of the person. Third, both the stereotyping process and contents of the stereotype are 'faulty' because the resultant stereotype is almost certainly an *inaccurate* picture of the real world. Finally, the *negative connotation* of stereotyping and stereotypes (that is, they are not good things) is further supported by the belief that they are *not flexible* and *not easy to change*. An implication from this view is that it is possible to make an association between an (inaccurate) derogatory stereotype and prejudice.

The commonly-held contents of stereotypes

One of the early studies of stereotypes, Katz and Braly (1933), established a paradigm for examining the contents of stereotypes:

the trait checklist. In 1932 one hundred students from the University of Princeton were given a list of eighty-four descriptive adjectives (e.g. intelligent, artistic, industrious, passionate, conventional, conservative). They were then asked to choose the adjectives that best described ten ethnic groups (these were nationalities such as Italian, English and German, along with Jews and blacks). Finally they indicated the five most characteristic adjectives for each of the groups.

The key result was the finding that there was a high degree of *consensus* between the participants in the study as to the characteristics of the group, indicating a common stereotype. The English were seen as *sportsmanlike, intelligent, conventional, tradition-loving* and *conservative*; and the Americans as *industrious, intelligent, materialistic, ambitious, progressive*. Subsequent replications of this study – in 1950 by Gilbert (1951), and in 1967 by Karlins *et al.* (1969) – have shown that many of the stereotypical traits were chosen consistently over a period of thirty-five years. For example, the perception of Germans as *industrious* was chosen by at least 50 per cent of the participants in all three studies.

The strong *consensus*, both across participants and across such a long time period, can be seen as support for both the inaccuracy and inflexibility of stereotypes. Indeed, Katz and Braly (1933) pointed out that the results indicated a failure of thought in that these stereotypes can only occur 'so long as individuals accept consciously or unconsciously the group fallacy attitude toward place of birth and skin colour' (p. 288–289). In their view these stereotypes were rigid views of others bearing little relationship to the actual facts.

However, the replications of the original study did show some evidence of change over time. The Japanese stereotype became more negative in 1950, presumably as a result of the Second World War. The negative stereotypes of Jews and blacks became more positive over time, indicating a possible impact of societal changes on the contents of the stereotype. Also, by the 1950s, the belief that it was wrong to stereotype had been promoted both in the media and amongst college students, and

Gilbert (1951) suggested that this was in part responsible for the reluctance of the students in his study to attribute stereotypical labels to the groups and for the reduced agreement between the students on the characteristics applied to the groups. Interestingly, the agreement between the students in the Karlins *et al.* (1969) study on the traits attributed to groups was higher than in the Gilbert study. In some cases this agreement was on different traits to those of the original study, indicating that a new consensus arose around a changed set of traits.

The 'faulty thinking' view of stereotyping

The dominant view, after Katz and Braly (1933), was that stereotyping is an inaccurate judgement and so the use of stereotypes is a 'failing' to think 'correctly', particularly as the contents of many stereotypes are derogatory (such as lazy or unintelligent) and so could be linked to prejudice against the group. The implication was that we should try and stop stereotyping, as it meant we did not see people accurately, but in a false and prejudicial manner. In 1971 Brigham summed up the view: 'most writers agree that stereotypes are undesirable and should be eradicated' (Brigham, 1971, p. 30).

Why are stereotypes false?

Essentially, in the fifty years after Lippmann's work, a stereotype was defined by many authors as an 'incorrect' generalization or overgeneralization (Brigham, 1971). Judging Italians as *artistic* (a stereotypical trait from Katz and Braly, 1933) implies that all (or most) Italians are perceived as artistic regardless of the actual number who are artistic. It is an overgeneralization. Furthermore, as Italians are viewed to be artistic without a consideration of the actual prevalence of artistic talent within the Italian nation, the stereotype is evidence of a 'faulty' thought process. Finally, it was argued that a stereotype is rigidly held. Thus, the stereotyped view is retained regardless of new information or changes in circumstances (Brigham, 1971).

Brown (1965) criticized the view that generalization on its own is a problem. He challenged the proposed reason that stereotypes are false because they treat 'a large number of distinguishable people as equivalent, it is a generalization and so ignores individual differences' (p. 176). To counter this view Brown uses the example of road traffic signals. Whilst each traffic light is a unique object, we treat each red light as the same, *for the purposes of traffic control.* We stop when the traffic light is red. We need to make the categorical judgement or else we would not be able to understand or predict the flow of traffic at a junction. Thus, Brown argues, categorical judgements can be very helpful in anticipating events. He goes further: 'It is a chief occupation of the human and animal mind to form categories to the end of discovering recurrence to the end of anticipating the future. We must generalize about categories and we ought to generalize about categories' (p. 177). So what is it that makes stereotypes problematic, unlike traffic signals?

First, whilst we can be pretty sure about traffic lights, we may not be able to judge the accuracy or inaccuracy of a stereotype (Brown, 1965; Brigham, 1971). If I claim that I am better at anagrams than you it is not too difficult to find a suitable measure of anagram-solving performance to compare us on. We might get a friend to organize a test of our skill and see which of us can solve more anagrams in a thirty-minute period. If the test is fair and the result clear then we will both agree whether I am correct in my original claim. However, consider a stereotypical trait such as Italians being artistic (Katz and Braly, 1933). What is a fair measure of artistic ability and how can we decide that Italians have more of this than English or Americans? There is no agreed measure of 'artistic ability' and no way of fairly comparing different nationalities. (This does not mean that we cannot *argue* the case either way. A person could argue that Italians are more artistic than others, citing Michelangelo and da Vinci. However, that does not mean that the counter-argument could not be equally well put.)

Brown (1965) argued that it is the cultural absolutism or ethnocentrism of stereotypes that makes them false. This is the belief that our (stereotyped) views are the correct way of viewing the world. We accept our cultural norms as being 'true' rather than a specific view within our culture. This results in the following false reasoning: we believe that group X are lazy *so they must be*. Campbell (1967) goes further in suggesting that the holder of the stereotype blames the characteristics of the group for the hostility he or she holds towards the group: *they may be poor but I do not think they deserve welfare support because they are lazy*.

A second problem of stereotypes picked up by Brown (1965) and Campbell (1967) is the assumption that the stereotypical characteristics attributed to a group of people are *inherent* to the members of the group: that is, the characteristic is in their nature. For example, the stereotypical characteristic of laziness might be used to explain why there are few business leaders from a particular ethnic group. Group members are seen as failing to achieve business success through their inherent laziness; thus ignoring the social and environmental conditions (such as apartheid laws, institutionalized prejudice or pervading attitudes) that have prevented members of the group from succeeding in business. Explaining the artistic brilliance of the Renaissance as due to the artistic 'nature' of the Italians ignores the social and historical factors completely (often referred to as the *Zeitgeist*).

Also this belief ignores the influence on the stereotype of the people doing the stereotyping. As we shall see later in the book, attributing characteristics to others may have more to do with the characteristics and culture of the people doing the stereotyping than the characteristics of the people being typed.

Campbell (1967) argued that the overlap between groups on a characteristic is not acknowledged by a stereotype. Assigning a stereotypical characteristic to one group is taken (erroneously) to indicate that *all* members of the group have this characteristic to a greater degree than the members of another group. The stereotypic belief that Italians are artistic might lead a holder of that belief to assume that all, or most, Italians are more artistic than, say, all, or most, English people, so that, if you were to take an Italian and an English person, the Italian would almost certainly be more artistic. However, this assumption is almost invariably false due to the overlap of the groups on the characteristic. Let us assume for the sake of argument that the Italians in general are really more artistic than the English and that we are able to measure accurately how artistic each person is. All this means is that the average 'artistic' score for the Italian people is higher than the average 'artistic' score for English people. However, any *individual* English person could be more artistic than almost all the Italians due to the range of scores in the two populations. Further, an averagely artistic English person could be more artistic than nearly half of the Italian population. (The question of how we reason on this type of information will be picked up in Chapter 3.)

Brigham (1971) concluded that all of these failures to think 'correctly' lead to a definition of stereotyping as a 'generalization made about [a] . . . group, concerning a trait attribution, which is considered to be unjustified by an observer' (p. 31). He goes on to say that 'the observers' have been the psychologists and sociologists undertaking the research. Thus, it is the researchers who define the criteria of what is a justified or unjustified attribution and, as Brigham (1971, p. 32) points out, these criteria are usually *assumptions* on the researchers' behalf. To Brigham, it was important for these assumptions to be made explicit for research to develop.

If stereotypes are false why do we hold them?

The question is: why are stereotypes so prevalent if they are false? If a stereotype is a false view of other people, why would we maintain them. One reason is motivational – stereotypes are a feature of prejudice. People may not be able to, or may not wish to, alter their stereotyped way of thinking, as it confirms their prejudiced opinions of others. Many of the early studies on prejudice within psychology focused on possible motivational reasons for a negative view of members of a social group.

Frustration and aggression

There are many occasions when we are frustrated in our actions, and it has been argued that frustration leads to aggression (Dollard *et al.*, 1939). A person who is frustrated in their career or personal development may not be able to direct their aggression at the cause of their frustration, either because it is too powerful – such as when someone is made redundant as a result of a business take-over – or unknown – such as when a person loses their job through a downturn in the world markets. But where aggression cannot be directed at the source of frustration, then another target might be chosen as a *scapegoat* (Secord and Backman, 1974). The person might direct their aggression at another social group who are a weaker target, such as a deprived ethnic group: *if it wasn't for them taking our jobs things would be fine*. Thus, through the redirected aggression the scapegoated group are seen in negative and stereotypical terms. In this view, examples of racist violence can be viewed as scapegoating due to frustration.

The authoritarian personality

An alternative motivational idea to the frustration–aggression model of prejudice came from the work of Adorno and colleagues on the *authoritarian personality* (Adorno *et al.*, 1950). They undertook an analysis of a wide-ranging set of opinions gained through a series of questionnaires. From this analysis they argued that the prejudiced person is likely to have a personality characteristic of *authoritarianism*, in that prejudiced people tend to be conventional, obedient to authority, to emphasize power and toughness, to eschew tendermindedness, to view the world as a dangerous and degenerate place, and they tend to suggest harsh penalties for criminals. Furthermore, the authoritarian personality tends to think in rigid stereotypical ways.

These researchers were primarily concerned with understanding why people were anti-Semitic (particularly in the light of the horrors of the Holocaust). The explanation of why the prejudiced person has this personality type can be given in Freudian terms. Brought up in an environment of strict discipline and parental authority, the resultant aggressive feelings about oneself or one's family do not have an expression and are repressed in the prejudiced person. In Freud's theory if emotional energy does not find an outlet it can undermine the integrity of the person, so the *ego* (the controlling part of the personality) redirects this energy to give it an outlet. These feelings are then *displaced*. Expressing anger towards powerful strict parents goes against the conventions of respecting and admiring one's parents and so the feelings are *projected* on to another source: a weaker social group. Thus, in this way, the authoritarian person continues to view their own social group (family, community) highly but projects these negative feelings on to other social groups who are seen as being unpleasant and aggressive. How does the authoritarian personality now explain why these groups are unpleasant and aggressive? Adorno *et al.* argued that the authoritarian personality is very concerned with power and status, interpreting the high status of their own social group (and the positive feelings they hold about it) as indicating an inherent superiority: *WE are good, clever people who deserve our position*. The negative feelings projected onto the low-status minority groups are then used to justify their position: *THEY are of low status because of their unpleasant characteristics and degenerate nature, THEY deserve to be treated badly*. Thus, the prejudiced group are viewed as unpleasant and aggressive because *it is in their nature* and so, to the authoritarian person, the prejudice is 'justified'.

A key characteristic of the authoritarian personality is rigidity of thought: that is, both in the stereotypical way in which they view other people and also in an intolerance of ambiguity. Thus, the prejudiced person rigidly maintains a view despite counter-evidence, and also rigidly separates ideas from one another, being unwilling or unable to accept that views such as *they are wily and if we don't watch out they will cheat us* and *unlike us they are not intelligent enough for management positions* are contradictory. (Later it was questioned whether rigidity of thought had been established in this research (Brown, 1965,

p. 508). Also, as we shall see in Chapter 6, the work of Billig has shown that the prejudiced person may be as sophisticated in arguing the case to maintain their views as the tolerant person.)

For the prejudiced person, holding a stereotyped view of other people has a motivational purpose. Repressed hostility to their oppressive parents is projected onto others, thereby maintaining their *social identity* as a person within a high-status social group, with high self-esteem.

Intergroup competition

Evidence that stereotyping might arise from group processes was shown by a famous series of studies by Sherif and colleagues (Sherif *et al.*, 1961; Sherif, 1966). They showed that hostility between groups emerged with *intergroup competition*. In a series of studies in a boys' summer camp, after an initial three days settling in, the boys were divided into two groups and competitions were set up between them. The boys developed a strong allegiance to their own group (giving themselves names – Eagles and Rattlers – and labelling their clothing with their insignia). Members of each group developed negative opinions of the other group as a result of the competition. These exhibited themselves in the shared dining hall where hostility broke out between the two groups. Only the requirement of group cooperation for a desired reward reduced the hostility in the latter part of the study.

Here the explanation is that intergroup competition for resources leads to hostility and prejudice between the groups. Whilst in the boys' camp the competition was for prizes, we can extrapolate to other groups such as tribes or nations where the competition is for land, water or other natural resources. Thus, prejudice is seen to arise out of a process of intergroup competition, which will occur when two groups wish to control the same limited resources. Furthermore, with the competition comes a negative view of the competing group.

All the explanations described so far imply a motivational origin to negative stereotyping. In response to frustration and strict upbringing we need to dissipate our built-up aggression, or in response to limited resources we must compete with other groups to survive. These responses lead to the negative views a person holds of other groups.

Our thinking is faulty

An alternative to the motivational reasons is a cognitive one. Stereotypes may reflect 'faulty' thinking and we may not be aware that we are making mistakes in our thinking about others. This cognitive view can be traced from the early work of Lippmann, described above, and Allport (1954). Allport argued that prejudice is 'an antipathy based upon a faulty and inflexible generalization' (p. 9), and so stereotypes arise from the categorization of the social world that provides these simplifying generalizations. Because stereotypes arise from *over*generalizations they are by their nature false (Allport, 1954).

Surely people realize, when they stop and think about it, that their stereotypes are false? One possibility is that people do not believe them to be false despite being told that they are. One early suggestion is that people assume that there must be some truth in such widely held views. Like the proverb *there is no smoke without fire*, researchers have asked whether there is not a 'kernel of truth' in a stereotype (Brigham, 1971): underlying the overgeneralization is there a core of basic evidence on which the stereotype is based? A person might argue: 'Surely there is some truth in the artistic nature of the Italians – look at Florence, Venice, Rome. What of Raphael, Michelangelo, da Vinci?' The problem is, as we saw above, that without a valid measure of artistic ability it is not possible to answer the question, particularly in referring to comparison groups such as the English. However, people might maintain their belief that there is 'truth' in the stereotype by drawing on highly memorable examples (see Chapter 3 on the availability heuristic).

Also, consider how we gain our knowledge of the world. Clearly one source of knowledge is our own experience. Yet researchers have found that people hold stereotypes of nationalities that they have not personally encountered (Katz and Braly,

1933). A second source of knowledge is through other people (Deutsch and Gerard, 1955). The importance of culture to our knowledge should not be underestimated. If we find a high consensus on a particular view of a particular social group – from our friends, acquaintances and the media – it is likely that we will accept this *normative* influence as the appropriate way to view the group.

It is quite possible therefore that, because a wide range of other people hold a particular view, we will stick with it. We can regard our knowledge of people and events as cultural, in that the views we hold are common to our culture and communicated between the members of it. At one time people believed that the world was flat. Now we would say that they are wrong, as we believe that the world is round. But in the past a person would have found it very hard to convince anyone that the world was round: *the people on the bottom would fall off!* Most people in their culture shared the view that the world was flat and the high level of consensus led to a high degree of confidence that the view was the 'truth'.

Telling people to stop stereotyping

If stereotyping is related to prejudice and is undertaken by prejudiced people or even if it reflects faulty thinking (that people may not appreciate is wrong) then it seemed appropriate to point this out to them and encourage them to stop stereotyping. Brown (1965) describes an advertising campaign in the media in the United States against ethnic stereotyping with its emphasis on the 'simple-mindedness' of stereotyped thinking. Posters, magazine articles and television messages all exhorted the public not to stereotype. As Brown (1965) points out, the campaign resulted in less public expression of stereotypes but it is quite possible that stereotypic beliefs were still privately held.

Taylor and Porter (1994) argue that the motivation of psychologists to persuade people of the 'evils' of stereotyping lay very much within the culture of the United States of America

GNITION AND CULTURE

of the research was being undertaken. A lot of the reotyping in America was focused on ethnic groups, ereotyping was seen as integral to racial prejudice. r and Porter suggest, the motive lay within the polit- ical ideology of the United States where peoples from different cultures were seen as being part of a cultural 'melting pot' producing Americans rather than remaining distinct groupings. Finally, Taylor and Porter argued that the research finding that similarity leads to liking led to the view that breaking down differences between groups would lead to more social cohesion within American society.

The cognitive approach to stereotyping

In the 1970s a number of authors began to question whether stereotyping arose from 'faulty' thinking as opposed to 'correct' thinking. It was suggested that stereotyping arose out of the processes of 'ordinary' cognition (e.g. Tajfel, 1969; Hamilton, 1979) which was neither 'faulty' nor 'correct'. Drawing on the cognitive ideas of Lippmann (1922) and Allport (1954) that as human beings we need to simplify and categorize the social world, it was argued that these are not mental failings (to be corrected) but rather features of the way human cognition operates.

This led to the question of whether the process of stereotyping was being viewed in a particularly negative way. Had researchers in viewing stereotyping as a 'bad' thing presented stereotyping itself in a particularly rigid way? Stewart *et al.* (1979) argued that the use of simple testing procedures such as ticking a list of traits and observing the level of agreement (consensus) had made stereotypes appear simplistic. Furthermore, the choice of ethnic and national stereotypes which can call up very strong emotions or opinions in some instances (such as opinions on race in the United States of America) or no personal knowledge in others (such as participants' knowledge of Turkish people in the early studies) meant that these were particular views that were unlikely to change very easily. Thus, the methods and the materials employed to study stereotyping could have made stereotyping appear overly simplistic and rigid (Stewart *et al.*, 1979).

Taylor and Porter (1994) also argued that, unlike the 'melting pot' of the United States, European or Canadian researchers worked in cultures where cultural difference was expected and locating people into different groups was normal. For example, Taylor and Porter suggest that cultural diversity is seen positively in Canada as a 'mosaic' rather than a 'melting pot'. This is not to say that these cultures do not have prejudice and ethnic disputes. Rather it is that the categorization process need not in itself be abnormal. Furthermore, stereotyping as a process need not be 'an inferior cognitive process' (Taylor and Porter, 1994, p. 88). Also, we can show by examples that stereotyping does not always lead to a negative view of a particular group: for example, the French are viewed stereotypically as romantic and cultured.

Categorization and schema

It can be argued that we need to categorize the social world in order to understand and interact with it. If categorization is fundamental to perception, in that we need to be able to distinguish chairs from tables to know where to sit and where to put a plate, then it will also be important in social perception. For example, we categorize one group of people as 'friends' as opposed to those people who are 'not friends'. This is important as we will engage in different behaviours with the two groups and have different expectations about their behaviour. Similarly we need to be able to distinguish the shop assistants from the customers in a shop if we are to successfully purchase something. Chapter 2 will consider the importance of categorization to human cognition. If categorization is fundamental to cognition then stereotyping may well be an outcome of the categorization process (Tajfel, 1969).

Categorization not only protects us from cognitive overload, in that we are simplifying the enormous amount of information available to us, but it also provides an organization of information about the social world (Hamilton, 1979). By classifying human beings into men and women we are able to allocate the attribute *able to have babies* to women and not to men. Thus, we can build up expectations about social events: the people having babies in a maternity hospital will be women rather than men. An important question is how we represent categorical information in memory. How do you distinguish between a friend and a non-friend? What information is contained in your concept of 'friend'? How is this information organized? One important theoretical concept that we shall consider in Chapter 2 is the *schema* (Bartlett, 1932), which is viewed as a cognitive structure that contains and organizes our knowledge about a category (Fiske and Taylor, 1991). For example, a schema for a 'chair' is an object with a seat and a back for sitting on. Most chairs have legs although some can have a solid base. In the schema we will also have information about the relationship of the attributes of the category as well as the attributes themselves. For example, we do not expect a chair to have legs as tall as a house with a small seat. If schemas are the way we store information about categories and concepts, then stereotypes can simply be viewed as schemas as well (Hamilton, 1979). For example, the schema for 'librarian' may include features such as *wears conservative clothes* and *introverted* as well as *stamps books and replaces books on the shelves*. Thus, stereotypes can be viewed as a feature of 'ordinary' cognitive processes and the organization and retrieval of information in memory.

Cognitive processing and stereotyping

Despite the proposal that stereotypes arise out of the normal processes of cognition we cannot deny that stereotypes do misrepresent members of the stereotyped category. A fashionably dressed librarian clearly does not fit into the librarian stereotype so will not match the expectation of the person holding the stereotype. So why is it that our cognitive processes lead us to have such expectations that will, in certain cases at least, be shown to be incorrect? In Chapter 3 we will be looking at the nature of human cognition. We shall consider how we make judgements about other people. It has been suggested that we are usually more strategic in our cognitive processing than logical or statistical, but that does not mean that people are not very good at social perception. Rather than seeing cognition as failing to come up to certain standards of logical or statistical accuracy we should view it in terms of whether it fits the requirements of the job of making sense of the social world. Fiske (1992b) argues that people are *pragmatic* in their social perception: our strategies are good enough to achieve the goals we want to achieve. Imagine a busy person with only a few minutes to take a book back to a library. They find the check-in desk empty and look around the room for a librarian. Who is a librarian? They might pick on a person who fits the librarian stereotype first. They might make a mistake but if they are right they will have solved their problem quickly and with the least effort. As we shall see in Chapter 3, strategic human cognition may employ stereotypes to make our thinking quick and easy.

Stereotypes in explanations

In Chapter 4 we shall consider how we explain events in the social world. Once again there is the question of whether people spend time thoughtfully attempting to work out the best explanation for an event or whether they rely on 'ready-made' explanations based on expectations and explanations contained within stereotypes. For example, consider the question: why did Doreen, the librarian, choose to stay at home and read a book rather than go to a party? There are lots of possible reasons: she did not like the party-giver, she was tired from going to many parties, there was no transport and so on. However, we might decide that she did not go to the party because librarians are introverted and bookish and prefer their own company to parties. Thus, we have not sought to find out further information to help our decision but have relied on a stereotype to guide our judgement. A stereotype will often contain personality or dispositional characteristics that provide ready-made explanations. Why did the college sports team captain fail his examinations? If we stereotype him as a 'jock', with the implication that he is not very clever, then his failure is stereo-typically attributed to his inferred lack of intelligence.

Intergroup perception

Stereotyping is essentially about the perception of groups. In categorizing someone as a member of a group we are then attributing the characteristics of the group to that individual. However, we should not forget that the perceiver is also a member of a social group. We are not isolated individuals unrelated to the other people around us pondering about them in a dispassionate manner. We exist as a member of a number of social groups. We are family members, we belong to occupational groups, we are a member of a nationality. In analysing groups, the group of which we are a member is referred to as the *ingroup*, and a contrasting group that we are not a member of is referred to as an *outgroup* (Tajfel and Turner, 1979). As we shall see in Chapter 5, we have a tendency to view an ingroup in more positive terms than an outgroup, and thus stereotypes may arise as a result, not just of individual cognition, but of a cognitive process of categorization and a motivational process of comparison. If we view outgroups stereotypically (*they are all the same*) and negatively compared to the ingroup (*they are less intelligent, hard-working, caring than us*) then it serves to enhance our *social identity* (Tajfel and Turner, 1979) – that is, the sense of self we gain from the group we belong to.

Stereotypes and language

In the last two decades there have been criticisms of the cognitive approach to social psychology both in its theory (focusing on cognitive mechanisms) and its methods (which are predominantly experimental). This has led to a critique of the cognitive explanations of stereotyping along with alternative methods being employed to examine the topic. The view that stereotypes are individual cognitive structures has been challenged (e.g. Potter and Wetherell, 1987). In viewing them as a feature of individual cognition it is argued that two crucial aspects have been lost. The first is the *social* aspect of stereotyping. We must not ignore or underestimate the nature of social interaction in use of stereotypes – which it is claimed that the cognitive approach appears to do. Second, stereotypes are expressed through *language*. We can only observe stereotypes through their linguistic expression. Rather than assuming that stereotyped language results from a particular cognitive structure, we can analyse the language itself: what people say to each other, what they read and write. Stereotypes occur as part of discourse. Rather than trying to seek causes of behaviour in terms of 'things in the head' we can analyse the different discourses employed by people around a topic, such as a particular social group. If we investigate the arguments that are used in discussion we find that prejudiced people are not more rigid than non-prejudiced people (e.g. Billig, 1985). People attempt to support their views through argument and prejudiced people will select particular arguments to maintain their views. So stereotypes will be employed as a device for maintaining an ideological position in an argument rather than as a result of some cognitive process of categorization. Furthermore, we find that people will employ a variety of different discourses in describing others (Potter and Wetherell, 1987) and do not rigidly stick to the one stereotypical description of members of a particular social group. Chapter 6 will focus on *discourse analysis* and the criticisms of the *social cognition* approach to stereotyping described in previous chapters.

Stereotypes and culture

A further criticism of the cognitive approach to stereotyping is that, in concentrating on individual cognitive processing, there may be a tendency to ignore the role of culture in stereotypes. In Chapter 7 we look at a theory that attempts to redress this balance. Much of our knowledge of other people does not come from personal contact with them but through other sources, be it chatting to a neighbour, reading a newspaper or a book or watching television. Children learn an enormous amount through their parents, teachers and friends, which they are not able to experience themselves. What we regard as 'common knowledge' can be seen as the shared knowledge existing within a culture. This will not only concern knowledge of the world (*the earth is round*) but also knowledge of people (*the French are good cooks*).

One attempt to capture the communicative and cultural elements in common knowledge is the theory of *social representations* (e.g. Moscovici, 1984). Our knowledge of things is viewed as culturally-based representations. Social representations are not just 'knowledge' in the head of the person, nor are they exclusively in spoken or written utterances, but like money they can be passed between the members of a culture. Through communication between group members, be it through conversation or the use of the mass media, social representations can be generated and passed within a culture. Thus, common knowledge is developed and transmitted. In Chapter 7 we shall be considering stereotypes as social representations.

Finally, in Chapter 8 we look at the different perspectives on stereotyping as different levels of explanation and consider how they inform us about a case of negative stereotyping.

Summary

Stereotyping is the attribution of characteristics to a person based on their group membership. Stereotyping has been viewed as inaccurate as it assumes all group members to be similar and ignores the variation between group members. A person may be discriminated against as it is assumed that they have the stereotypical characteristics of their group. Psychologists have proposed motivational and cognitive explanations of stereotyping. Currently a cognitive explanation is the dominant approach. However, in recent years the importance of language and culture has been considered more fully in the understanding of the psychology of stereotyping.

Further reading

Hunyady, G. (1998) *Stereotypes during the decline and fall of communism*. London: Routledge. An interesting book examining stereotyping in Hungary, giving a historical perspective over a time of social change.

Lippmann, W. (1922) *Public opinion*. New York: Macmillan. Like the writings of William James (1890), Walter Lippmann's book is very readable and packed full of intriguing ideas. Despite its age it is well worth seeking out to compare the theories of modern researchers with Lippmann's views.

Chapter 2

The categorical perception of people

Introduction

WHEN WE SEE AN OBJECT or a person do we apprehend it in its full rich *individuality* or uniqueness or do we see it as a member of a particular *category* of object or person? Do we combine the characteristics of an object in a piecemeal way in perception – the shape (*it is round*), the size (*it is small*), the colour (*it is red*), the movement (*it is bouncing along the ground*) – or do we perceive it in some form of overall, global perception (*it is a ball*)? How do we perceive people? Do we combine all the knowledge we have about them to form a composite impression (*quiet, likes to be on their own, doesn't like parties*) or do we assign them a category label (*introvert*)? This is a key question in the psychology of person perception as it is assumed, in viewing someone as a particular *type* of person, or indeed in *stereotyping* them, that we are not viewing them in terms of their idiosyncratic characteristics (*has a particular interest in orchids, has a birthmark on the left arm*) but finding the category into which to slot them (*old man*) with all the implications contained in the categorization. Placing something in a category can be seen as going beyond the information we have about that thing, and it allows us to make inferences based on our knowledge of the category. For example, what can you infer about a small, brown, hairy, four-legged creature with a tail? However, if you label it a 'dog' you are likely to infer that it will bark and certainly not

30

meow. Similarly with a person: will our categorization lead us to make inferences about other characteristics of him or her? But first we shall consider the evidence for the categorical perception of people.

Categorization in the perception of objects

That perception is a process of identification or recognition has been argued within psychology for well over a hundred years. As William James noted: 'Thus, I hear a sound, and say "a horse-car"; but the sound is not the horse-car, it is one of the horse-car's least important manifestations' (James, 1890, p. 78). Many years later the psychologist Bruner claimed that 'all perception is necessarily the end product of a categorization process' (Bruner, 1957, p. 124). The linguist Lakoff is equally certain: 'There is nothing more basic than categorization to our thought, perception, action, and speech' (Lakoff, 1990 (1987), p. 5). In this view, perception is essentially a process of classification and only when I categorize an object or an event do I give it meaning. A particular pattern of sensation will fall upon my eyes and ears, yet I will perceive it to be a ball bouncing on the ground. It is the categorization of the object as a 'ball' that gives the sensations a meaning.

When I categorize an object by the concept 'ball', I can then distinguish it from other objects and use my knowledge of the category to make other judgements concerning it. I can tell you also the difference between a rock and a football. I know that one is hard and dangerous and that the other is inflated and used in a game. If I see one flying towards me I will choose to avoid it if I perceive it to be a rock and I will try and kick it if I perceive it as a football. This ability to place objects and events into conceptual categories is seen as crucial to cognition:

> Why is the ability to categorize such an integral and central part of cognition? Try to imagine a world in which we did not treat objects such as chairs as members of conceptual categories. One problem is that each object which we in fact perceive or 'see as' a chair would be seen as a novel object

– we would be unable to *recognize* or *make sense* of such perceptions because we would have no common label to attach to them. Thus the ability to place objects in conceptual categories is a fundamental property of *perception*.

(Roth, 1986, p. 19)

This view proposes that without this ability to categorize we could not function. We need to decide what is a chair and what is not a chair so that when we go into a room we can sit on the right thing. Without being able to distinguish between tables, chairs, walls and floors the world would be an impossible place. The neurologist Sacks (1985) gives an example of a patient with a form of anomia, that is, a loss in being able to name certain objects and hence being unable to recognize them. This loss made his life very difficult. Sacks gave him a glove and asked what it was. The patient could describe its form but was unable to identify it: '"A continuous surface," he announced at last, "infolded on itself. It appears to have" – he hesitated – "five outpouchings, if that is the word"' (Sacks, 1985, p. 13). He simply could not recognize what it was or decide on its function, despite Sacks' prompting that it might fit part of the body.

Born to categorize?

Studies have shown categorization very early in life. For example, a 2-week-old child can distinguish between a human voice and other sounds (Wolff, 1966) and a 1-month-old can distinguish between syllables such as 'ba' and 'pa' (Eimas *et al.*, 1971). Goren *et al.* (1975) showed that new-born babies, only 9 minutes old, could distinguish between drawings of faces and non-faces made up of the same features. It appears that as human beings we have an innate propensity to recognize the human face.

Learning categories

Much of a child's early life involves learning conceptual categories and we observe this through language acquisition. Language learning involves both vocabulary (learning the meaning of words) and grammar (putting words in the correct order and choosing their correct form). We can view learning the meaning of words as the learning of conceptual categories. An adult gives a young child a soft red ball and says 'ball', a word they do not recognize. Let us consider this from the child's point of view. The child presumably accepts that the adult is communicating something to them, but the problem is what does the sound 'ball' refer to? What aspect of the situation is 'ball'? There are many possibilities. 'Ball' could refer to the object, its roundness, its colour (*does 'ball' mean 'red'?*), its texture, its softness. It could even mean 'gift'. This is a cognitive problem for the child: what does the word 'ball' mean?

It has been proposed that young children may employ a number of constraints in their relating of words to categories in order to make the task more feasible (Pan and Gleason, 1997). They list five of these assumptions or hypotheses that it is proposed the child employs: words refer to objects, words refer to whole objects, new words refer to categories that do not already have a name, no two words have exactly the same meaning, each object can have only one name. Thus, 'ball' (probably) refers to the round thing.

Children develop a knowledge of 'things' through categorization but the child's use of a concept might not initially match that of the adult definition. My own children when very young could say that 'daddy works at the university', but that did not mean that the word 'university' had the same meaning to them as to an adult. In the early phases of learning children might employ an *overextension* and extend the concept beyond the adult use, such as calling all small animals 'dogs' or all men 'daddy', or use an *underextension*, restricting the concept to fewer items than the adult term, and, say, call only the family car a 'car'. For the 2-year-old child these forms of category extension will occur commonly in their speech (as much as a third of words) but will occur much less in the following year (Clark, 1993).

Essentially, children are developing their knowledge of categories through a process of induction: that is, generalizing from the collection of personal experiences they have had. For example, an adult points to a small four-legged creature in a park and says to the child 'dog'. On another day in the park the child sees a different four-legged creature – this time it is bigger and of a different colour. The child points at it and says 'dog'. The adult says 'yes, a dog'. The adult has confirmed that this second creature is also a dog. From the child's point of view the question is: what are the *characteristics or features* that make it a 'dog'? It is clearly not the colour or the size as these have differed across the two examples. The child must reason out what defines the category dog. It has been suggested that we use *similarity* to categorize (Bruner *et al.*, 1956), so we might decide that two objects are in the same category if they look the same or serve the same function. Similarity of appearance appears to underlie the overextensions mentioned above. Thus, the child might decide that any small four-legged creature is a dog. Thus it is through the process of perception that we develop our knowledge of the category 'dog'. Goldstone and Barsalou (1998) have argued recently that it is perceptual processes that underlie most of our concepts.

However, when the child sees a cat and points at it and says 'dog' (an overextension) the adult replies 'no, that is a cat'. This new experience is a problem for the child: it must redefine the category 'dog'. Through the combination of encountering different animals, plus the *feedback* from the adult, the child over time gains a wider range of experiences of what is, and what is not, a dog. Adult feedback, especially with additional information about the key features of an object, can be very useful in helping a child with an overextension (Chapman *et al.*, 1986). Interestingly, however, it is worth noting here that even as adults we might not be clear in what defines a category. Can you write down what distinguishes a dog from a cat? We might tell a child that birds can fly but later they learn that ostriches and kiwis are birds which cannot fly. Also, not all concepts are of equal complexity and it is easier to define a concrete concept like 'chair' than an abstract one like 'justice'. Furthermore, we can see that many categories are not clearly defined at their boundaries: when does a dish become a plate? when is a house a cottage?

Later on in life the child may be given the formal defining characteristics of a category of objects, such as mammals, in a biology class in school. Here it is not personal experience that has led to concept learning. Rather it is *cultural transmission*: knowledge of the concept has been communicated through other people. Then the child will be asked to *deduce* which animals in a list are mammals and which are not, that is, infer from the general defining characteristics which specific items fall into the category. Having learnt that mammals have hair or fur and suckle their young, the child will be able to deduce that a dog is a mammal and a crocodile is not.

Categorization in the perception of people

If we categorize in order to perceive objects then we can ask whether the same processes operate in perceiving people. Do we learn about categories of people, with their characteristic features, from personal experience and learning from others? It has been argued that, with certain provisos, person perception follows the same processes as object perception (Taylor *et al.*, 1978; Fiske and Taylor, 1991). If this is the case, do we share the same views about types of people as we do about objects in our world?

Personality types

It is tempting to hope that, if there are different categories of people, then we should be able to determine what those cate-gories are. Just as there are different types of furniture to sit on – chairs, stools, benches, sofas – we can ask whether there really are different types of people in the world. It would certainly simplify the complexity of perceiving people. It would help us to predict and explain the behaviour of other people if we could identify them as belonging to a type. We could use our knowl-edge of that type of person to say who would be brave and who would be cowardly, who we would like, who would enjoy parties, who would make good leaders and so on. Rather than being completely unpredictable any individual would fall into a particular category with known characteristics. If this were the case, all we need to do is identify the different *personality types*. If we knew which type of person someone was then we could use our knowledge of that type of person to predict how they would perform in different situations, and they would no longer be unknown.

Throughout history, people have held this belief and have attempted to discover the number and nature of human types, often based on radically different assumptions concerning the reasons for the different types. For example:

- The Greek physician Galen, in the first century AD, based his system of person categories on amounts of four body fluids, arguing that if we had an excess of a particular fluid then we would tend to a particular personality type. There were four main types of people: sanguine, melancholic, choleric and phlegmatic, based on the fluids: blood, black bile, green bile and phlegm. Thus, the melancholic person is suffering from an excess of black bile and the choleric person from green bile. More importantly, labelling John as melancholic means that his general sad disposition isn't going to make him much fun at a party. Also, if Susan is choleric, then being quick-to-anger and passionate she might not be the best person with whom to discuss politics.

- Western astrologers have placed us into twelve broad categories, corresponding to the position of the sun in the zodiac at our birth. Thus, the natal position of the heavens influences our personality. 'Ah yes,' my friends say to me, 'as an Aquarian you were bound to be interested in people so no wonder you became a psychologist.' Chinese horoscopes identify each year with an animal, so those born in the Year of the Horse will have a different personality to those born in the Year of the Rat.

- In the field of psychology, Sheldon (1942) argued that there is a relationship between body type and personality, with three major body types: endomorphic (rounded and fat), mesomorphic (muscly and athletic) and ectomorphic (thin with little muscle). Each person's body lies within these extremes and your personality tends towards that of the body shape you fit best. Thus, the endomorphic person tends to be sociable and even-tempered whilst the mesomorph is bolder and more aggressive with a desire for power. The ectomorph tends towards introversion and is more highly strung.

- Jung argued that people had either an introverted or extro-verted attitude to experience, and Eysenck has incorporated the introvert–extrovert dimension as a key feature in his personality theory where introversion–extroversion and neuroticism–stability are the key dimensions. To Eysenck the differences between people on introversion–extroversion depend on physiological differences in the brain (Brunas-Wagstaff, 1998).

We can certainly dismiss the validity of typologies based on false premises such as melancholia being a result of an excess of (non-existent) black bile, or 'criminality' being based on the features of a woman's face as Lombroso and Ferrero (1896) proposed at the end of the nineteenth century. Furthermore we can question whether *any* typology is adequate as a psychological explanation of human personality (Mischel, 1968, 1973). Indeed, within the field of Personality Psychology the question of whether it is theo-retically valid to identify a set of different types of people is one of the key questions (e.g. Brunas-Wagstaff, 1998).

Impression formation

So, there is still the question of whether we see people in categorical terms despite the possibility that there may not be a fundamental set of personality types inherent within the human race. When presented with information about a person do we gain an overall, categorical, impression of that person or do we judge each piece of information separately and inde-pendently, gaining an impression from their composite characteristics? This has been studied under the heading of *impression formation*.

Thorndike had observed as far back as 1920 that if a person judged another highly on one particular personality characteristic, particularly one involving a good–bad judgement, they might also rate the same person highly on a range of other characteristics. This was termed the *halo effect* (Thorndike, 1920). For example, in interviewing a candidate for a job you might find the person very likeable and easy to talk to. You rate them highly on 'communication skills'. You might also rate them highly on intelligence, motivation and conscientiousness despite not having gained information on these characteristics. It is as though the initial high rating creates a general impression of the person as 'a good candidate' and this halo influences other judgements of them. The halo can work the other way. A candidate rated as bad on one characteristic might be rated badly on a range of other characteristics. It is as though the initial judgement produces an overall impression of a 'good guy' or 'bad guy' and this influences subsequent judgements.

The Gestalt psychologists, also working in the first half of the twentieth century, argued that perception has a quality that is more than simply the sum of the individual elements of the experience. A classic example is a melody where the psychological experience is more than simply the sum of the individual notes. Our experience has an overall shape or form (a Gestalt) that is not contained within the individual elements; the tune is not contained within the separate notes. Asch (1946), working within the Gestalt tradition, examined the impression gained from a personality description. Asch gave his participants a list of seven personality characteristics, such as *intelligent, skilful, industrious, warm, determined, practical, cautious.* He then asked them to look at a checklist of additional personality characteristics and tick which ones they thought the person would have as well. From this he found that the person in the above list was viewed as a generous, good-natured, sociable sort of person. One of his manipulations was to change a characteristic to its opposite in the initial list of seven and to see the effect that this had on the checklist items ticked. He found that with certain personality characteristics, such as changing *warm* in the above list to *cold,* it had a major effect on the checklist. The impression gained by the list *intelligent, skilful, industrious, cold, determined, practical, cautious* led to the person now being seen as ungenerous, unhappy, irritable, unsociable. Simply changing *warm* to *cold* in the list had had a major effect on the overall judgement. Thus, the effect of a change of one word in the list of seven was to change the overall Gestalt of the person: it didn't simply change a seventh part of the impression. Changing other characteristics, such as *polite* to *blunt*, had much less of an effect on the characteristics ticked on the checklist.

Asch termed characteristics such as warm–cold as *central traits*, in that they appeared to be central to the overall impression of the person, and characteristics such as polite–blunt as *peripheral traits*, as they appeared to be peripheral in the overall judgement. Thus it appeared that the impression gained was not a simple combination of the traits but an overall Gestalt: that is, the relationships between the traits were considered and integrated to give the overall impression. Further support for this came from other studies he undertook with the same paradigm. Consider the list *kind, wise, honest, calm, strong*. Here the initial traits lead to an overall impression where 'calm' is interpreted as serene, and 'strong' as fearless and noble. Now consider this list: *cruel, shrewd, unscrupulous, calm, strong*. Here the impression leads to the interpretation of 'calm' as cold, and 'strong' as ruthless and hard. Asch pointed out that the meanings of traits were influenced by surrounding traits, with the central traits having most influence. Also, traits early in the list influenced the interpretation of ones later in the list. The impact of this *meaning change hypothesis* is that the overall judgement is of a global, organized and consistent form. Notice how the description *kind, wise, honest, calm, strong* produces an overall judgement of a character that we might label as 'noble'. As Kunda *et al.* (1997) showed, when given a category it can strongly influence our interpretation of a characteristic, so, for example, learning that a lawyer is aggressive conjures up a different impression (argues, competitive) from that conjured by knowing that a construction worker is aggressive (gets into fights, rude, impatient).

Anderson (1965) disagreed with Asch's interpretation of how impression formation operates, arguing that an overall impression arises from the 'piecemeal' combination of traits. He suggested that each trait has a value on a certain dimension, such as like–dislike, and the overall impression from a list of traits is a weighted average of their values. Thus *happy* has a higher value than *severe* on the dislike–like scale and it may also carry more weight in the overall impression. This weighted average model was able to explain much of the data without requiring the meaning change hypothesis of Asch (see Hinton, 1993).

So, do we form global impressions (Asch) or combine information in a piecemeal manner (Anderson) along a particular dimension? Support for Asch's view came from studies of impressions gained from apparently conflicting information. Asch and Zukier (1984) presented participants with descriptions such as *brilliant* and *foolish*, which appear opposite on the unintelligent–intelligent scale. But the participants combined them by viewing the person as *academically brilliant* but *foolish in terms of a lack of common sense* (such as an absent-minded professor). To make sense of the information they had considered *brilliant* on the intellectual–unintellectual scale and *foolish* on the worldly–unworldly scale. Thus, they had not viewed the traits on the same scale but multidimensionally. Similarly, Casselden and Hampson (1990) showed that participants combined the traits *cruel* and *kind* not on a simple dimension (such as good–bad) but by seeing them as aspects of the same person: *this person is cruel but they may appear kind*. One trait was seen as the real or inner persona and the other as a guise or outer persona. Thus, it appears that impression formation is often an active case of trying to make sense of the characteristics in an integrated way to give the person an overall character rather than just combining them on a single dimension according to some mathematical averaging process.

It has been suggested that in forming an impression of someone we are trying to place the person into a 'person category' we already know. What we try to do is draw from the available information that which is most diagnostic of the cate-

gory (Skowronski and Carlson, 1989). Knowing that someone is *warm* is more helpful in fitting them to a category than knowing that they eat lunch. Skowronski and Carlson (1989) showed that often negative information (such as: *stole from his friends*) is more diagnostic than positive information (*likes animals*). Support for 'negativity bias' (the greater weight given to negative information) operating at the categorization stage of processing has come recently from work by Ito *et al.* (1998). How these person categories are represented mentally is discussed below.

The organization of knowledge of person categories

Why do we form these categorical impressions of people? So far we have seen that through perceptual experience and information from other people we develop our knowledge of conceptual categories. What is of interest now is how the information about these person categories is organized, how we are able to make these multidimensional judgements that someone who is *cruel but kind* is superficially kind but really cruel inside.

Implicit personality theory

You and I may agree on what is a chair or a tree but we may have different views on what makes a 'friend'. From my own experience of people I might have developed my own view of personality types and the categories of people that I am likely to meet. These 'naive theories' of personality were termed *implicit personality theories* by Bruner and Tagiuri (1954). My implicit theory of personality is the set of interrelationships and associations between personality characteristics that I understand to be the case. I may view a 'friend' as a person who makes me laugh with silly jokes, likes to chat over a drink in a bar and enjoys going to football matches. From my experience these are the people I choose as friends and the people who are my friends have these characteristics. You, however, may have a very different view on what constitutes a friend. We may have a range of differences in the way we view people. I might see Bob as a fun guy and you might view him as an irritating jock. Furthermore, when we use terms like 'fun' or 'friendly' we may using them to refer to very different characteristics. Your definition of 'friend' might include characteristics such as enjoys country walks, classical music and animals – which is very different to my view described above.

An influential theory that offers an explanation of how our implicit theories of personality form is Kelly's *personal construct theory* (Kelly, 1955). Kelly argues that, like a scientist, we want to be able to predict and understand people and events in the world. Experience guides the way we *construe* (view, understand) people and events. And how we construe people and events guides the way we experience them. We are in a constant cycle of experience and construction. Consider the example of starting at college or beginning a new job. You meet a large number of new people who all begin as unknown and hence unpredictable individuals, but experience of them leads you to discriminate between them; one group of people are now viewed as 'friends' whilst the rest are 'not-friends'. Now you have identified a group as friends you view these people in a different way to the non-friends. And that makes them more predictable. If I construe John as a 'friend', then I predict he will help me out when I need a favour. If he doesn't, then, like the scientist, I might question my construction of the situation. Is John really a friend? Am I asking too much of my friends? Should I change my view of what makes a friend?

A 'friend' here is what Kelly terms a *personal construct*: it is my personal understanding of a category of people or events and it has developed out of my repeated experience of different people. Kelly proposes that every construct has two *poles*: in categorizing a set of people as 'friends' I am contrasting them with another set of people (the 'not-friends'), so happy–sad, male–female, likes-parties–does-not-like-parties are all constructs. The same word might be used in more than one construct. If I am contrasting friends with acquaintances then the construct is friends–acquaintances (rather than friends–not-friends). I might also use the word 'friends' in another construct 'friends–enemies', which is a different construct to friends–acquaintances. Also,

constructs may not have a simple verbal label: for example, those-people-who-make-me-feel-all-tingly-inside.

According to Kelly, constructs are combined in a hierarchical system, with some constructs subordinate to others. Constructs higher up the hierarchy characterize the way a person views the world in general terms. If I am strongly attached to my region of the country and it is a positive higher-order construct (I view my region and all things to do with it very positively) then the construct 'friend' will be subordinate to it. When I use the term 'friend' it contains the implicit view that only people from my region can be classed as friends. As another example, Rosenberg and Jones (1972) analysed the descriptions in a book by American author Theodore Dreiser and found that the three concepts, male–female, hard–soft and conforms–does-not-conform, underlay many of his descriptions. There was a close relationship of male to hard and female to soft in his implicit personality theory. In Kelly's terms the male–female construct was high in the construct system. The construct system is our personal way of viewing the world and is a complex system of the associations between constructs. It is a framework through which we construe the events and people around us: it is our knowledge system through which we view the world.

So do we develop idiosyncratic beliefs about people and objects given that we all have different experiences? The answer is: to some extent but there are reasons why our views tend to be similar. We share many similar experiences with other people and these common experiences lead to common ways of viewing people and events. My experience of 'shopping' or a 'party' may be very similar to yours if we share the same culture. But we should also remember that in categorizing a person or object (in construing an event), we often check our judgement with other people. Just as the child learns from the adult's feedback what is a dog and what is a cat, so we frequently get feedback on our own judgements. We ask other people what they think. Indeed we may change our perception of events to conform to those of other people (Asch, 1956). The adolescent who has spent many happy times watching trains might have developed the belief that train-spotting is fun and is something friends do together. However, feedback from a group of new friends at school might lead him to question this construction of events. They tell him that they think train-spotting is boring. He might conform to the majority view and reconstrue train-spotting as dull and boring, or he might stick to his original belief and reconstrue the new friends as 'not-friends'. Indeed, Kelly worked as a counsellor at a university and noted how people's personal problems often related to an unsuccessful or inappropriate construction of events. If one student construes another as 'best friend' but is in return construed as 'an-OK-person-on-my-course' then there will be differences in expectations about the relationship and one of them may be surprised or upset by the actions of the other.

Interestingly, Bieri (1955) showed that *cognitively complex* people – those who used a large number of constructs – were better able to predict the behaviour of others than *cognitively simple* people who used few constructs. The cognitively simple person is unable to fully match the behaviour of others with complex descriptions and hence construes others in a relatively simplistic way – what we can regard as a stereotypical manner.

Prototypes

It had been suggested that an object is defined by certain key characteristics (Bruner *et al.*, 1956; Collins and Quillian, 1969). Thus a chair can be defined as *a seat for one person with a back*. Characteristics such as *has four legs* or *is made of wood* are features of many chairs but are not defining characteristics, as we recognize as a chair one that has a box base with no legs or one made out of plastic or metal. However, Rosch (1975) has argued that some objects are more typical of a concept than others. For example, a robin is viewed as a more typical bird than an ostrich. Furthermore, people are quicker at categorizing a typical object than an atypical object (Rosch, 1973), so will respond faster that a robin is a bird than that an ostrich is a bird. Also, categories often have 'fuzzy boundaries' – it is difficult to decide if a particular object is in one category or another. A chair with a small

back might be classified as a chair by some people and as a stool by others. To explain these factors Rosch suggested that we store information about concepts in *prototypes* (Mervis and Rosch, 1981), that is, in terms of the abstracted features of most typical examples of the category. So when I ask you to think 'chair' you will bring into mind a prototypical chair. This will not be an actual chair that you remember but the 'model' of a chair you have in mind that best represents the category chair. The typicality effect indicates the sort of chair this model or prototype is: it will be closest to the real chairs you recognize most quickly. Rosch and Mervis (1975) suggest that prototypicality is determined by looking for *family resemblances* between category members: the more characteristics an object shares with other category members and the fewer it shares with members of different categories, the more prototypical it is.

Cantor and Mischel (1979) suggest that our categorization of people follows Rosch's model of the categorization of objects. When deciding what type of person someone is we will consider three factors: how many of the category characteristics do they have? (*breadth*); to what extent do these characteristics stand out from their other characteristics? (*dominance*); and do they have characteristics incompatible with this category? (*differentiation from other categories*). So John is more of a 'swot' (keen, hardworking student who prefers studying over other activities) than Peter, even though they both do well in examinations, because John is always asking the tutors questions and studying in the library but Peter has more of a social life. When we have limited knowledge of a person we will look for the central or important characteristics of the type: does John stay in to study rather than go to a party?

Mayer and Bower (1986) showed that people could learn a person prototype from particular instances. They made up a personality type from sixteen characteristics. Participants read descriptions of sixty people (thirty of whom were in the category and thirty who were not) and had to decide after reading each description if the person was in the category or not. Then they were told if they were correct or not. Accuracy rates were over

45

70 per cent for the last twenty descriptions indicating that the participants had learnt the prototype.

Schemas

An alternative proposal for representing object and person categories in memory is the concept of a *schema* (Fiske and Taylor, 1991). This concept comes from the work of Bartlett (1932) on memory. Barlett found that people's memories of events were sometimes distorted by their understanding of such an event. For example, if I am trying to remember your birthday party I might recall that you blew out the candles on a birthday cake even though you didn't this year. The explanation is that I use my schema to fill in the gaps in memory. My schema for 'birthday party' is my knowledge (my mental representation) of a birthday party, including all the features of it such as the person whose birthday it is, birthday cake and candles, balloons, presents, singing happy birthday and so forth, along with the relationship of the features to each other (e.g. we only give the presents to the person whose birthday it is). As another example, I might find it horrifying to learn of a group of people in masks surrounding an unconscious man who is having his chest cut open by one of them. However, if I know that the people are 'doctors' and 'nurses' and that the unconscious man is a 'patient', then I can evoke my 'hospital operating theatre' schema and make sense of the situation. Furthermore, I would be shocked to find that the person doing the surgery was a nurse rather than a doctor, as I know from my 'doctor' schema and 'nurse' schema that it is the doctors who do the surgery. A schema can influence the way we interpret new information, remember information or make inferences about people and events (Fiske and Taylor, 1991).

Fiske and Taylor (1991) argue that we have social schemas to represent our social knowledge. One type of social schema is the person schema, so the information we have about a friend will be organized as a schema and we will use our schema to make sense of information about them: *Mary is an introvert so I don't think she will like John who is rather outgoing and loud.* Similarly, we can have schemas for categories of people, such as an 'accountant' schema or a 'footballer' schema. Fiske and Taylor (1991) term these *role schemas*. An important point they make is that a role can be an *achieved role*, where the role is achieved by the person, such as becoming a doctor or member of the town council, or an *ascribed role*, which is attributed to us on the basis of a characteristic (such as our gender, ethnicity, age, height) which is not one we have acquired by our own actions. Other people will have schemas for teenage girls or middle-aged men which lead them to interpret individuals and their actions in specific ways: 'One can think of stereotypes as a particular kind of role schema that organizes people's expectations about other people who fall into certain social categories' (Fiske and Taylor, 1991, p. 119).

Prototypes and schemas

Prototypes and schemas are sometimes used interchangeably but there are differences between them (Fiske and Taylor, 1991). A prototype of 'male movie star' might be something like Tom Cruise, with a touch of Tom Hanks and Keanu Reeves. Even though it is an abstraction a prototype has all the features specified: it includes youngish and clean-shaven as well as playing the hero in blockbuster movies. However, the schema for male movie star does not require all features to be specified – only the defining ones, such as playing the action hero and being a romantic lead. Sean Connery clearly fits into the schema of male movie star even though he is older than the three actors mentioned above and is often bearded. Also, the schema concept focuses more on the relationship between the important features of the category rather than constructing a prototypical instance. But, as Fiske and Taylor (1991) point out, there is a large overlap between the two concepts as they are both abstract representations of categories.

Prototypes and exemplars

It has been argued that exemplars may be more important than abstract representations such as prototypes when we perceive other people (Smith and Zárate, 1992). In the above example, Tom Cruise, Tom Hanks and Keanu Reeves are all exemplars of the 'male movie star' category. When faced with an actor such as Sir Anthony Hopkins how do I categorize him? It is suggested that I make my decision on the basis of the exemplars that are brought to mind. If my exemplars are Sir Laurence Olivier and Sir John Gielgud I may type Sir Anthony Hopkins as a 'great British actor'. If Sean Connery and Michael Caine are brought to mind I may classify him as a 'male British movie star'. My categorization depends on the exemplars that come to mind, so another actor might be categorized as a 'Sylvester Stallone–Bruce Willis' type of action hero. Exemplar-based perception is seen as more flexible than abstract prototype-based perception, as each new person is typed according to their own features and the exemplars these features activate. However, it implies that we are creating a new type with each new person, so this may be an inefficient form of perceiving people, as well as being unable to explain evidence of more abstract categorizations. Furthermore we need a more abstract category such as 'male actor' – otherwise how would we know which exemplars to bring to mind (Sherman, 1996)?

Which categories of people do we use?

Given that we do categorize people, there a number of different categories into which we can place any individual. Each of us has numerous characteristics. The following is merely a sample of one individual's attributes: a 30-year-old married woman, with short, dark hair, who works as a doctor, drives a Volkswagen car, enjoys playing tennis and listening to jazz. So which category do we place this particular person into?

Rosch (Rosch *et al.*, 1976; Rosch, 1978) argues that there are certain *basic level categories* at which knowledge is organized. In changing level from specific to general these are the categories which are the most general whilst still retaining the overall similarity of group members as well as an overall prototype for the category. For example, the categories Chippendale chair, chair, furniture are increasing in generality but chair is the basic category because it is a higher level than Chippendale chair and the similarity between chairs allows us to form a prototypical chair. Furniture is too general for a basic level category, as the similarity between members (chairs, beds, cupboards) is less than for the category, 'chair' and it is difficult to conceive of a single prototype that represents all 'furniture'. We can see this with person categories as well. The category 'people in employment' is rather too general a category, whilst 'teacher of geography in a private school' is too specific. Thus a category such as 'teacher' may be a basic level category and hence more commonly used. It has been suggested that basic level categories are the ones first used by children (see Lakoff, 1990 (1987)).

However, depending on the circumstances, certain categories will be more *salient* than others. Even when a person is a stranger there are certain characteristics that we immediately observe, such as their age, ethnicity, gender, height or body shape. Visual characteristics such as clothing and hair style will often be readily available. Also the context in which we observe someone may lead us to focus on a certain characteristic. The one woman in a room full of men may lead us to focus on her gender in categorizing her (Taylor *et al.*, 1978) as it is that characteristic that is *distinctive*. Certain categorizations may be particularly salient to us, either because they are ones we use often (see implicit personality theory above, p. 41), or because they have been recently 'activated': having seen a television programme on youth and crime we might tend to categorize a young man climbing over a fence as a delinquent.

Oakes *et al.* (1991), following Bruner (1957), argue that the salience of a category depends on *accessibility* and *fit*. Certain categories will be more accessible than others depending on the *motivation* for the perception and state of the perceiver, such as trying to find an assistant in a large store or looking around at a party for a potential partner. The match between the observed characteristics of the person and those of the category is the measure of fit. A person wearing a uniform standing behind a counter is a better fit to the store assistant than someone dressed in casual clothes carrying shopping bags.

Roles

Sometimes we don't want to know what people are like, we just want them to do something for us. We are interacting with these people for a specific purpose: we want to buy something from the shop assistant or ask a police officer for directions. We are not really interested in them as individuals, nor in getting to know them 'as people', but only interested in terms of the *role* they serve. We expect shop assistants to describe the goods on offer and engage in the process of assisting our purchase. As we categorize them according to their role, we have expectations about their actions. When these expectations are fulfilled then our interaction with them operates to our mutual satisfaction. If we do not have these *role expectations* then there can be a breakdown in interaction. If we didn't expect shop assistants to take our money for the goods we might end up being arrested by the store detective!

Clearly, treating people in terms of their roles can result in a successful interaction. However, we often go 'beyond the information given' (Bruner, 1957) and give personality types to occupational roles. A bank manager might be seen as responsible and concerned with money, and nurses as kind and helpful, because of our tendency to see behaviour as emanating from personality characteristics rather than the requirements of the role (see Chapter 5). Notice that the inference we are making here is that a particular type of person takes on a particular type of role. If someone is a librarian we know the job is sedentary, working indoors with books in a quiet environment, requiring the ability to catalogue and offering little scope for noisy conversation. What type of person would want to do this? Clearly not an athletic person or a gregarious person. We are likely to infer that a typical librarian will be an introvert, probably not sporty, who likes books (and so enjoys reading, which is a solitary pursuit). Thus we have constructed the 'typical' librarian from the role they have undertaken. This need not be viewed as a stereotype, as a typical librarian does not exclude a range of other characteristics within the category of librarians: a librarian could be athletic or extroverted, but they are not typical characteristics (just as an ostrich is still a bird even though it is not as typical a bird as a robin). It becomes a stereotype when we assume that *all* librarians are introverted.

Conclusion: why categorizing people is useful

Whilst it may not be psychologically valid, it does appear that people find it very useful to label others as a particular type, such as introvert or typical Aquarian. Consider a man, John, who likes to spend time on his own, either reading or walking. John does not like parties and is quiet and shy of other people. He spends hours on his hobby repairing and restoring old watches. How do you describe John to others? I have used nearly forty words, yet if I had described him by the single word 'introvert' you would have known what I meant. Indeed, the words extrovert and introvert are now part of our everyday vocabulary with very few people employing them in terms of Jung's theory. We don't need to. Labelling someone an introvert is immediately understood by others: an introvert is quiet and prefers their own company to that of others. It is a useful way of describing a particular person rather than listing out all their preferences and dislikes or describing their behaviour. Thus, categorization may well be an *efficient* way of dealing with information about people (as we shall examine in the next chapter).

Summary

It has been suggested that we need to categorize objects in order to perceive them. Categorization appears to play an important role in person perception too. Through our own experience we may develop an individual view of people, an implicit personality

51

theory, but through the similarity of our experiences with those of other people and the influence of others within our culture we are likely to develop similar contents of person categories. This knowledge about person categories may be stored in memory in the form of prototypes or schemas which we can then employ in perceiving other people.

Further reading

Fiske, S.T. and Taylor, S.E. (1991) *Social cognition.* 2nd edition. New York: McGraw-Hill. The classic account of social cognition.

Kelly, G.A. (1963) *A theory of personality – the psychology of personal constructs.* New York: Norton. A readable theory of how we make sense of people and events through personal constructs.

Lakoff, G. (1987) *Women, fire and dangerous things. What categories reveal about the mind.* Chicago: University of Chicago Press. The title says it all!

Chapter 3

Cognitive processing and stereotyping

Introduction

THE VIEW THAT HUMAN cognition is not able to apprehend
the full complexity of the world has been a central tenet in
much of the work on stereotyping since Lippmann (1922) first
argued strongly that a stereotype is a simplified picture of the
world. The focus of this chapter is the way in which human cognition operates. What is the nature of human cognition and in what
way is it limited? In what way do the limitations of cognition
lead us to make categorical and stereotypical judgements.

Furthermore we can ask the question: can we decide to override a stereotype and try to re-evaluate information on an individuating basis?

We need to simplify to perceive

Through the work of a number of key researchers (e.g. Lippmann, 1922; Allport, 1954; Bruner, 1957; Tajfel, 1969; and Hamilton, 1979) the role of cognition has been emphasized in stereotyping. As we have seen in the previous chapter, we employ a process of categorization to deal with the enormous amount of information we receive about objects and people. The categorization process also operates in social perception. However, categorization is also a simplification and the simplification is required because of the limitation of human cognition. It has been argued that the reason we need to simplify (categorize) is to prevent *cognitive overload* (Hamilton and Trolier, 1986). That is, our minds are not capable of dealing with more than a certain amount of information at any one time: we are limited in our mental processing capacity.

We have a limited mental capacity

In the 1950s a number of psychologists argued that human cognition has certain limitations, a key one being that we are *limited capacity processors*. A crude interpretation of this is that we are not able to perceive, attend to, think about, or respond to more than a certain amount of information at once. If there is more information available than we can take in it simply gets ignored. We shall see below that this original view has been modified over time, but we will consider one or two studies that led to this belief.

Crossman (1953) asked people to sort a deck of cards into different piles, such as red and black or suits. When people tried to do this as fast and as accurately as they could he found a clear relationship between the sorting time and the number of sorting

55

categories. It took longer to sort the pack into four categories (suits) than two categories (red/black). But, more importantly, he found that the graph plotting the time to sort the pack against the number of categories (expressed in information units called 'bits') was a straight line. This implied a *constant rate of information transmission*. We can explain this as follows. If you fill up a small bucket with water from a tap turned on fully it will be quicker to fill than a large bucket. What you cannot do is make the water flow through the tap any faster (it's on full) or make the size of the tap bigger (it's made of metal). The water is flowing through the tap at a constant rate. If we imagine our cognitive processing to be analogous to the tap, then a constant rate of information transmission means that we have a 'mental processing system' of *limited capacity* (the size of the tap) and we can only deal with a certain amount of information at once (the flow of water). When we are presented with a harder task such as sorting the pack into four piles (a larger bucket) it will take us longer than sorting it into two piles (a smaller bucket). The linear relationship between time and difficulty was found in a number of tasks and was termed the Hick–Hyman law after the two researchers who studied it in the 1950s (see Welford, 1967).

We find it difficult to deal with more than one source of information

Also, at the same time, Cherry (1953) examined what he termed the cocktail party phenomenon, which is the ability, in a noisy environment such as a party, to select and attend to one conversation and ignore all the others around us. In his experiments participants wore headphones and listened to a different message being played to each ear. They were required to attend to one of the two messages (the attended message) by repeating it aloud. What Cherry (1953) found was that participants could recall much of the attended message (implying that it was being fully processed) but almost none of the unattended message beyond its physical characteristics (such as whether it was in a male or female voice). Broadbent (1958) explained this, and a number of other findings, by a model of human cognition in which a limited capacity information processing system was protected from overload by a selective filter. Whilst we are bombarded by many sources of information, only one can get through the filter to the processing system at any time, all others being filtered out. The filter uses the physical characteristics of the message (such as its location) to select it. For example, it is easier to attend to one of two people talking when they stand further apart than when they are close together. To attend to a different information source the filter has to be switched to it.

Subsequent research showed, however, that unattended information was not always filtered out. Moray (1959) showed that we can recognize our own name when spoken on an unattended message, and Treisman (1964) showed that when the unattended message was identical to the attended message but slightly delayed the repetition was detected. She also found that participants, in repeating back one message, would sometimes switch to the other message, without realizing it, if it made more sense to do so. If the message 'The footballer kicked the ball into the net' swapped from the attended to the unattended ear, after the words 'kicked the', the participant might continue to repeat back the sentence even though it had switched to the unattended ear. This led Treisman (1964) to suggest that the filter does not completely block all unattended messages but only attenuates them. It is as though the attended message is on a clear telephone line and the unattended message is on a noisy line – some information may still get through.

Kahneman (1973) argued that we should also look at task difficulty in deciding whether we are able to process two sources of information at once (e.g. do two things at once). We can do two tasks together if they do not exceed our limited capacity to process information, such as having a conversation whilst walking, but not if they exceed the capacity, such as writing a psychology essay at the same time as playing chess. A simple task takes up less of our mental capacity than a complex one, so tapping a finger and talking is easy to do, as tapping a finger is an easy task leaving most of our mental capacity for the conversation. However, there are people who can perform two apparently complex tasks at the same time, such as driving a car and talking about Einstein's theory of relativity or juggling whilst balancing a spoon on the end of their nose. How can these be done without overloading our mental capacity? The answer is *practice*.

Practice can lead to automaticity

Shiffrin and Schneider (1977) showed the effect of practice in a series of experiments. Participants were asked to remember a set of letters and then respond as quickly as possible whether one of these 'target' letters had appeared in a particular display. The responses of the participants were monitored over thousands of displays. The researchers examined the effect of the number of target items, the number of items in the display, and, most importantly, the 'consistency of mapping'. In a consistent mapping condition, letters would only appear in the display as target items to be detected and numbers would always be the 'distractor items' to be ignored. In a varied mapping condition, both targets and distractors were letters and a target letter to be detected in one display could be a distractor to be ignored in another display.

In the varied mapping condition the task took longer the more target items and the more items in the display. This required a 'serial search': checking each item in the display against each item in the target set. Shiffrin and Schneider argued that this task required attention. With consistent mapping, the task was much less affected by the number of target items or the number of items in the display. With practice the target items seemed to pop out of the display regardless of the number of targets to be remembered or items in the display. This was explained by proposing that the task was performed *automatically*. The development of automatic processing was shown when one set of letters were used as targets and a different set of letters as distractors in the consistent mapping condition (Schneider and Shiffrin, 1977). At first, performance appeared to be a serial search, but over two thousand trials performance became automatized. As a neat twist the researchers then switched the target and distractor sets of letters. This had an enormous effect. Participants were worse than at the beginning of the experiment. Having learnt to automatically detect one set of letters it took them a long time (another couple of thousand trials) to unlearn it.

The two-process view of human information processing

These studies of attention (along with those of Posner and Snyder, 1975) led to the view that we have two distinct forms of mental processing.

The first, developed from the limited capacity processing system of Broadbent (1958), is *controlled or conscious attention*. This system is of limited capacity, it takes time to operate and is affected by the difficulty of the task, taking longer when more information has to be dealt with. However, it is flexible and can deal with novel problems and involves conscious awareness. It also takes effort. For example, writing this book takes a conscious effort. Conscious attention is what we might regard as our thinking ability, involving paying attention, concentrating, focusing the mind on a problem and puzzling out what to do. It is thoughtful processing. When someone explains a difficult problem to me or I am weighing up different arguments then I am engaging my conscious attention. It is intentional, in that it is under my voluntary control. I can choose to think about a problem or not.

The second form of processing, *automatic processing*, does not use up our processing capacity, operates quickly, is inflexible and is unconscious. It also appears to operate effortlessly. As it does not take up attentional capacity we are able to perform automatic tasks at the same time as performing a task using controlled attention. But automatic processing relies on highly practised techniques or overlearnt expectations. It is also unintentional, in that it operates outside our conscious control. For example, due to your highly practised reading skills you cannot stop yourself reading a word when you see it (even if you wanted to). As an example, look at the following word but do not read it: CHAIR.

Consider the novice driver. At first, it seems impossible to engage the clutch as well as changing gear at the same time as holding the car steady on the road. I remember my own experience of this, thinking how effortful it was and how I had to do so many things in such a short time. Initially, conscious attention was required for the new tasks. Now, many years of driving experience later, I am hardly aware of changing gear at all, and can discuss complex issues of psychology at the same time (at least on a familiar road in daylight). Changing gear has become automatic through practice.

The cost of automaticity

Essentially, it is argued that when we are presented with a situation we can either engage in thoughtful consideration of the information available to us (pay conscious attention) or we can rely on learnt expectations or highly practised responses and engage in automatic processing. Whilst practice leads to automaticity and automaticity allows us to carry on more than one mental task at a time, there is a cost. The automatic task will be dealt with inflexibly and we are unable to deal with novelty when processing automatically. As Treisman (1988) argued, attention is required to 'glue' the features of a event together; without it we may make a mistake. Consider waiting at a traffic signal for the light to change to green. If we are not paying attention we might suddenly notice a green light and start off – only to realize that the green light is not from our traffic signal. When paying attention we are not as likely to make this mistake.

Applying the two-process model to social cognition

This two-process model of mental processing has been applied to social psychology by a number of researchers (see Chaiken and Trope, 1999), and we will see it in a number of studies concerning stereotyping discussed below. Two examples of this are Langer's (1978) research into *mindful* and *mindless* thinking, and Petty and Cacioppo's (1985) *Elaboration Likelihood Model* of persuasion.

Langer (1978) found that people would comply with a minor request quite readily, without consideration of the reason, but a larger request led to people paying attention to the reason for the request and only complying if they accepted the reason. In the first case, the request was minor so a person didn't think about it *mindfully*, assuming *mindlessly* that people usually have a good reason for asking a favour (because we have learnt that they usually do). A larger request, which put a person to some inconvenience, led to that person considering mindfully the reasons for the request before deciding whether to comply or not.

Petty and Cacioppo (1985) argued that we can be persuaded by the *central route*, which involves a thoughtful consideration of the issues involved. In this way we might buy a car from a retailer because we have considered the alternative makes and models and it best suits our needs on all the key factors such as price, comfort and fuel consumption. On other occasions we might be persuaded by the *peripheral route*, where learnt expectations or simple strategies such as 'don't miss out on a bargain' can be used to persuade us. We might buy the first car we see because the salesman takes us aside and offers us another 10 per cent off if we buy it now. Only later do we find out to our regret that the car is not suited to our needs and that the salesman offers everyone else 10 per cent off as well. In this theory of persuasion, the more likely you are to elaborate (think or consider carefully), the less likely you will be to be persuaded by the peripheral route. However, when the likelihood of elaboration is low, such as when you are distracted or in a hurry, then the more likely you will be to be persuaded by learnt expectations like 'fair's fair': this person has apparently done me a favour (such as giving me an extra 10 per cent off or throwing in a toaster for free) so I owe them a favour back and should buy the product (which later you may realize you don't really need or want).

Thinking about people and things

Do we think about things logically?

Much of the work on reasoning has shown that we are not always logical in the way we think (Wason, 1966). To reason logically we must take into account all possibilities before we can decide what must or must not be the case. For example, if I tell you that *some academics live in Oxford* and *some people in Oxford cycle to work* then you might be tempted to conclude that *some academics living in Oxford cycle to work*. This may be the case in reality but it does not *logically* follow from the first two premises. The reason is this. Imagine there are 100,000 people living in Oxford and 1,000 of them are academics and 2,000 of them cycle to work. It is logically possible that none of the 1,000 academics cycle to work. It could be the case that all of the 2,000 people who cycle to work are not academics. So *logically* we cannot conclude that *some* academics living in Oxford cycle to work. Logic is not about what really happens in the city of Oxford but is about what we can definitely conclude or not conclude from certain premises. This makes logic sometimes hard for us to understand, and when we are asked to reason logically we may not do so, and instead rely on 'real world' knowledge, such as *I know an academic who lives in Oxford and she cycles to work* (see Scribner, 1977), or a rule of thumb, such as *the word 'some' occurs in each of the two premises so I think 'some' should be in the conclusion* (Woodworth and Sells, 1935), or our stereotypical view of Oxford academics which involves them cycling through the historic town with a gown flapping around them.

Johnson-Laird (1983) argued that rather than employing logical reasoning we often use *mental models*, which are the models we hold in our heads of the way things operate in the world. So if my television breaks down I might fiddle with the on/off switch because in my simplistic mental model of a box with buttons that's the thing that makes it go on. Someone with a more sophisticated mental model of a television might try other things to find out what is wrong. A television repairer in a workshop with the proper manuals and circuit diagrams should be able to work their way through all the possibilities to definitely find out what is causing the problem.

A mental model can be seen as our schema of the object or event, and our thinking as a schematic inference. Using a schema saves us time and effort compared to trying to work out the logical answer. Making an inference from a schema to make a decision can be seen as a form of heuristic decision making, which we shall turn to now.

Do we think about things statistically?

What are the chances of snow this year? What is the divorce rate in this country? Is there a greater danger for a child walking to school or being driven by car? Who is more likely to be attacked in the street: a young man or an elderly woman? These are all questions which rely on our knowledge of statistics or probability. Consider a young woman contemplating whether to walk home or take a taxi from a friend's house one evening. She just wants to return home safely. How does she think about her choice? She could check the crime statistics for her town and find out how many young women have been attacked on the way home at that time of the evening, and evaluate the risk. She might also check the accident figures for crashes involving taxis. Then she chooses the one with the lower risk. She might even find the risks so low that she decides to see how she feels on the night. In this way she is basing her decision on statistical probability. Alternatively, she could do none of this but recall a rather vivid television programme about a horrific attack and decide that she will definitely take the taxi.

The work of Kahneman and Tversky (Kahneman *et al.*, 1982) has shown that when we make judgements under conditions of uncertainty we often do not take into account the statistical probabilities but rely on a *heuristic*: a 'rule-of-thumb' strategy that we have learnt. In one study of Kahneman and Tversky (1973) participants had to decide on the profession of someone from a personality description that they were told came from a group of 30 engineers and 70 lawyers. The participants made their decisions on the stereotypicality of the description rather than the odds. If the description fitted a stereotypical engineer the participants said it was an engineer even though the odds were 70 to 30 in favour of it being a lawyer. Kahneman and Tversky termed this decision strategy the *representativeness heuristic*. When the description was completely neutral, containing no stereotypical information about either profession, the participants said there was a 50 per cent chance that the person was an engineer, indicating that they were basing their judgement on the information in the description (which could equally be from a person in either profession) rather than the *base-rate information* which favoured the lawyers by 70 to 30. Further evidence that stereotypes rather than statistical probability influenced people's decisions was shown by other studies (e.g. Tversky and Kahneman, 1982; Fischhoff and Bar-Hillel, 1984), indicating that stereotypes can be viewed as heuristics (Bodenhausen and Wyer, 1985; Pratto and Bargh, 1991).

Tversky and Kahneman (1973) identified a second heuristic: *the availability heuristic*. Here we rely on the information that is readily available to memory when making a decision rather than the base-rate information. The availability heuristic can be said to have guided the woman taking a taxi home rather than walking due to the vivid memory of the television programme about a horrific attack. The base-rate information that the risk of being attacked is extremely small is not taken into account in the judgement. Similarly, Tversky and Kahneman (1973) suggest that the availability heuristic might lead us to infer that the divorce rate is rising if a number of our friends have just divorced (even though the countrywide divorce rate might be going down).

Illusory correlation and stereotype formation

Stereotyping involves the association between certain characteristics and particular groups, such as *caring* with nurses and *ambitious* with lawyers. There is the possibility that people observe real differences between groups (Judd and Park, 1993), and maybe there is a predominance of caring people in the nursing profession, but, as we saw in Chapter 1, it is very difficult to know if there is a 'kernel of truth' to a stereotype, particularly for characteristics we are not able to measure.

It is even more puzzling why a stereotype might arise where a characteristic, such as *criminality*, becomes associated with a particular group even when there is no difference in the prevalence of the characteristic in group members compared to other relevant groups or the general population. A cognitive explanation of this comes from Hamilton's work on *illusory correlation* (Hamilton and Gifford, 1976; Hamilton, 1979). A correlation arises when two things vary together. For example, there is a correlation between height and foot size: taller people tend to have larger feet and smaller people smaller feet. An illusory correlation arises when people believe there is a correlation when there is not.

In a study by Hamilton and Gifford (1976) participants read statements about the actions of people from two groups A and B, such as *John, a member of Group A, visited a sick friend in the hospital*. There were twice as many statements about people from group A as there were about those from group B, making people from group B more *distinctive*. There were also nine positive statements for every four negative ones, making negative statements more *distinctive*. A key point to note was that the balance of positive to negative statements about group A members was the same as for group B members. The participants were then asked to say who had performed a set of actions: a person from group A or group B. Results showed that they overestimated the number of negative actions performed by members of group B: they had made an illusory correlation between negative actions and group B members. In a second study, where positive statements were more distinctive, an illusory correlation occurred between positive statements and group B members.

As Hamilton (1979) points out, this has implications for the stereotyping of minority groups in society. If we (the majority group) rarely encounter members of the minority group we may make an illusory correlation if we happen to see a person from this group perform a distinctive act. After watching a news item about a minority group member having committed a murder (a distinctive event) we may associate this group with violent crime, despite the fact that they are no more likely to commit such a crime than a member of the majority group. Distinctive events attract attention and are likely to be better remembered (Hamilton *et al.*, 1985) which may well distort our judgement of the frequency of an event (as we saw above with the availability heuristic).

It is worth noting that illusory correlations do not always occur. In a study by Haslam *et al.* (1996) the two groups were either group A and group B, as in the earlier studies, or right-handers and left-handers. Negative behaviours were more distinctive than positive behaviours in the study. They found the usual illusory correlation between minority group B and negative behaviours. However, there was no illusory correlation between the minority left-handers and negative behaviours. This was explained by the participants' prior expectations: they did not expect a difference between left- and right-handers on the positive and negative behaviours. Thus prior knowledge may 'override' the formation of an illusory correlation.

Why do we think heuristically?

We should not infer from the above research that people cannot think logically or statistically. It is certainly something that we can learn to do: the psychologists undertaking the research have had to do it. The two-process model favoured by many researchers argues that we can think *systematically* as well as *heuristically* (Chaiken *et al.*, 1989; see also Chaiken and Trope, 1999). The question is: why do we often choose to think heuristically instead of systematically?

Thinking is effortful: we are cognitive misers

Fiske and Taylor (1991) argue that, due to our limited processing capacity, human beings act as *cognitive misers*. To put it simply, we do not like to think – it takes time and effort:

so [people] take shortcuts whenever they can. People adopt strategies that simplify complex problems; the strategies may not be normatively correct or produce normatively correct answers, but they emphasise efficiency. The capacity-limited thinker searches for rapid adequate solutions, rather than slow accurate solutions.

(Fiske and Taylor, 1991, p. 13)

We often rely on what has worked in the past and seems to work now. As Robertson (1999) points out in his review of research into human thinking, even when we have all the information to consider a problem in detail our capacity limitation might mean that it is too much information to deal with and we still get the answer wrong! We rarely have the time or the inclination to ponder each new problem of our daily lives and so quick decisions without too much effort may have much pragmatic value to us.

Prejudice and the unfinished mind

The title to this section comes from a paper by Fox (1992a). Fox, picking up from the findings of Kahneman and Tversky, argues that heuristic, intuitive thinking has real evolutionary survival value over probabilistic thinking. He drew on the science fiction television programme *Star Trek* for one example, arguing that, if faced with a sabre-toothed tiger, the logical half-Vulcan Mr Spock would have been killed as he pondered the odds of being attacked by the animal, whilst the human Captain Kirk would have whipped out his phaser and shot it. Fox argues that 'automatic' stereotypical thinking has evolved as a part of human cognition:

The essence of stereotypical thinking is that it is fast and gives us a basis for immediate action in uncertain circumstances. But its legacy is that we are happier and more comfortable when thinking in ways that promise immediate survival than in ways that appear to threaten it. This may no longer make much sense, but unfortunately our brain doesn't know that, or, if it can be persuaded of it, it still has a hard time bucking a system that got it to this point in the first place. Presented with the need for a quick decision, it will prefer stereotype to logic.

(Fox, 1992a, p. 140)

Fox argues that, since Lippmann's use of the term, stereotype has acquired a negative connotation that extends to all forms of prejudgements. Stereotyping is viewed as indicating a flaw in human nature, 'as evidence of the unfinished mind' (Fox, 1992a, p. 148). However, according to Fox, the focus on 'offensive prejudice' and our desire to remove it has meant that it has not been appreciated that stereotyped thinking is fundamental to much of human thought and that mostly our 'prejudiced thinking' is defensive in form, that is, it serves to protect us from the unfamiliar and, in evolutionary terms, enhance our chances of survival. Thus, he concludes, we cannot stop stereotyping as it is not a defect of thinking. 'We have to come to terms with the idea that prejudice is not a form of thinking but that thinking is a form of prejudice' (Fox, 1992a, p. 151). We cannot eradicate stereotypical thinking as it is fundamental to us, but we can change the contents of specific stereotypes to a more positive view.

Not surprisingly, Fox's controversial article stimulated much discussion which was documented in the same issue of *Psychological Inquiry* as his own article. A range of criticisms were directed at Fox's thesis: for example, his implication that stereotyping is in some sense 'benign' (Devine and Sherman, 1992). Lewis (1992) argued that we should focus on the social relationships between people rather than on the nature of mental processing in order to fully understand prejudice. Both Fiske (1992a) and Neuberg (1992) emphasized the circumstances in which we do not rely on stereotypes for our judgements. We shall examine these below. In his reply to the range of criticisms offered, Fox (1992b) argued that the heuristic thinking process of stereotyping has been too closely linked with the negative aspects of prejudice rather than considered in its overall position as integral to human thinking.

The use of stereotypes in cognitive processing

Stereotypes are processed quickly and efficiently . . .

Andersen *et al.* (1990) combined stereotype or trait categories (such as *politician type* for a stereotype and *extrovert type* as a trait category) with mundane acts (e.g. *closed the door*) or states (*became tired*). Participants had to respond yes or no to the likelihood of the type of person doing or experiencing the act or state and the response times were measured. The responses to the stereotype sentences were faster than those for the trait type sentences, which was interpreted by the researchers as indicating a greater efficiency in the processing of stereotypes.

Sherman *et al.* (1998) explain that, in their view, people are not cognitive misers in the sense that they use stereotypes to avoid effortful thought. Rather they use stereotypes to allow them to direct their cognitive 'resources' efficiently. The use of stereotypes offers a way of interpreting not only stereotype-consistent information (knowing Bob is a *priest* means his kind act is understandable in terms of the stereotype of a priest) but also stereotype-inconsistent information (we can direct our attentional resources to consider unexpected information such as Bob, a *priest*, committing an unkind act).

. . . so we use them when under pressure of time or information load

Gilbert and Hixon (1991) showed that, as long as a stereotype has been activated, then a 'cognitively busy' person is more likely to apply a stereotype than a less 'busy' person. Participants in the 'stereotype activation phase' of their study completed word fragments, such as POLI_E, shown by an Asian assistant. Some participants had to rehearse an eight-digit number at the same time to make them busy. The non-busy participants completed the fragments with a higher number of stereotypically Asian words, e.g. POLITE. In the 'application phase' the participants listened to the Asian assistant describing mundane life events.

69

Again some participants were kept busy by asking them to perform a visual task of detecting letters on a screen at the same time. The participants who were not busy in the activation phase and were busy in the application phase rated the assistant as more stereotypically Asian on a set of traits.

Macrae *et al.* (1993) also studied 'busy' participants who had to rehearse an eight-digit number to increase 'cognitive load' whilst watching a videotape of a woman describing herself. Some participants had been told that she was a doctor and others that she was a hairdresser. The busy participants rated her in a more stereotypical way than participants who had not had to remember the number.

Further support for the efficiency of stereotypes under 'busy' conditions came from Macrae *et al.* (1994). Participants were given a person's name (Nigel, John) followed by a list of ten personality characteristics which they knew they would be asked to recall later. The key manipulation was that half the participants were given a stereotype label with the name (Nigel-doctor, John-skinhead). Five of the personality traits were consistent with the stereotype (e.g. *caring* for doctor) and five were neutral. At the same time as forming the impression of the person described, the participants had to perform a second task (listening to a tape giving geographic information) which they were also to be tested on. The results clearly showed that the participants who had been given a stereotype label not only recalled more traits but also answered more questions on the geography information than participants without the label. Macrae *et al.* argued that this indicated that the efficiency of processing stereotypes acts as an 'energy saving' device to free up limited cognitive resources for other tasks.

We can see this in action in a study by Pendry (1998). Student participants were asked to form an impression of a 65-year-old woman by concentrating on information provided about her. At the same time an audiotape was played of a conversation about either a supermarket or a Student Union having to close. The conversation was not mentioned in the instructions but it was assumed that the participants would 'eavesdrop' more on the

Student Union conversation as it was a topic of relevance to them. Indeed, the students in the 'Union' condition did better in a test of their knowledge of the conversation. Also their ratings of the woman were more stereotypical of an *elderly woman* those of participants in the 'supermarket' condition. Stereotyping the woman had apparently allowed the participants to better eavesdrop on the conversation.

The automatic activation of stereotypes

An influential study examining stereotype activation in terms of the two-process theory is that of Devine (1989). In her first study white participants were asked to generate characteristics of the stereotype of blacks. The participants were also tested for their level of prejudice. The results showed that both high- and low-prejudiced individuals were equally aware of the features of the black stereotype. In a second study a number of words relating to the black stereotype were flashed on a screen in front of a participant to *prime* (activate) the stereotype, but too briefly to recognize. Following this the participants read a twelve-sentence paragraph about 'Donald' who was described performing ambiguously hostile behaviours, such as demanding his money back on an item he had just bought in a store. The subsequent ratings of Donald's hostility were influenced by the priming words, indicating the effect of the automatic activation of the stereotype, for both high- and low-prejudiced participants. In a final study, examining controlled processing, participants were asked to anonymously list their thoughts about blacks. Here an effect of prejudice was found, with low-prejudiced participants listing more positive than negative thoughts and more belief thoughts (such as *all people are equal*) than traits (such as *musical*), while the reverse was the case for the high-prejudiced participants.

Devine (1989) argued that all the white subjects knew the stereotype of blacks, all had been automatically influenced by it in the judgement of 'Donald', but that low-prejudiced participants consciously suppressed the automatically activated stereotype in the listing of their thoughts. This implied that all the participants had learnt the negative stereotype but, like breaking a bad habit, it was possible to consciously make an effort to replace it with non-prejudiced views.

In a word categorization task, Dovidio *et al.* (1997b) presented a subliminal image of either a black face or a white face prior to the presentation of the word to the white participants. They were interested in the speed of categorizing three positive traits (good, kind and trustworthy) compared to three negative traits (bad, cruel and untrustworthy). The results showed that, even though the participants were unaware of the faces, they categorized a negative trait word more quickly when it followed a black face and a positive trait more quickly when it followed a white face. This indicated an automatic activation of implicit (i.e. unconscious) racial attitudes. However, when asked to make a judgement as a pretend juror in the case of a black defendant, the participants' decision was associated with their overt or explicit racial attitudes (as found by questionnaires) rather than with their response times in the categorization task, thus supporting Devine's view of a dissociation between automatic and controlled racial attitudes.

However, we need to be careful, as the effects of automatic stereotype activation may be quite complex. Dovidio *et al.* (1997b) did find a relationship between the response times and nonverbal behaviour (blinking and eye contact) when the participants engaged in a discussion with a black person as part of their study, implying a subtle nonverbal link between automatic activation and behaviour. Indeed, contrary to the 'dissociation view', Wittenbrink *et al.* (1997) found a relationship between the implicit racial attitudes (from a word judgement task subliminally primed by the words *black* or *white*) and explicit racial attitudes measured by a questionnaire. Also, Lepore and Brown (1997) found that, even though both high- and low-prejudiced participants knew of the stereotype of black people and there was evidence of automatic stereotype activation for both groups (when presented with negative words linked to the stereotype), in one study only the high-prejudiced participants showed an automatic activation of the stereotype in response to the category *black people*. Lepore and Brown (1997) suggested that the low-prejudiced participants may have broken the bad habit and the stereotype is not automatically activated on the activation of the category *black people*.

Automatic social behaviour

Can the automatic activation of a stereotype have an effect on a person's behaviour? In one experiment by Bargh *et al.* (1996) participants performed what had been shown to be a very boring task – judging whether there was an odd or an even number of circles on a computer display. After 130 trials the computer displayed an error message telling the participants of a failure to save their data and that they would have to start the experiment all over again. The participants were videotaped and their level of hostility to learning they would have to do the experiment again was rated. The key manipulation was that prior to each trial a face was shown subliminally on the computer screen. Consistent with Devine's findings, participants who had been primed with a black male face showed significantly more hostility than those primed with a white male face.

In another experiment, participants had to make sentences out of sets of words displayed to them. One group of participants were shown words related to the *elderly person* stereotype (e.g. old, lonely, grey, forgetful). In an intriguing manipulation the researchers timed the participants walking down the corridor after completing the study. They found that the participants primed with the elderly person stereotype walked significantly more slowly along the corridor than control participants who had been give different words! Furthermore, when asked, none of the participants realized that the words they had seen were drawn from the elderly person stereotype.

Dijksterhuis *et al.* (1998) performed a variation on the 'elderly person study'. After the sentence completion task, the Dutch student participants were asked to fill in a short questionnaire about Princess Julianna, the 89-year-old Dutch Queen

Mother. In this study, participants given the elderly exemplar of Princess Julianna, after the automatic activation of the elderly person stereotype, walked more quickly than those given a neutral questionnaire about Belgium. Dijksterhuis *et al.* explain the two sets of results as indicating that the automatic activation of the elderly person stereotype in the Bargh *et al.* study had led to an *assimilation* effect of the stereotype on the walking behaviour, so participants walked more slowly. However, the presence of an elderly person exemplar (very different from the participants themselves) had led to a *contrast* effect on the walking behaviour, and participants walked faster.

The conditions of stereotype influence

Information about a person will not always be interpreted in stereotypical terms, despite subliminal or other priming. Consider the impression formed from the information: *the old woman found it difficult to get up*. This is likely to be interpreted in terms of the *elderly person* stereotype if the perceiver has been primed by words like *frail* or *infirm*. But three conditions are required (e.g. Banaji *et al.*, 1993). First, the stereotype must be *accessible*: we must know it and it must be retrievable from memory. Second, the information needs to be primed by a trait such as *frail* that is relevant to the behaviour, as this has *applicability* to the *interpretation* of the behaviour (as *frail* is associated with the risk of falling over but *lonely* is not). Third, the priming needs to have *applicability* to the *social category* (*frail* is a stereotypical characteristic of elderly people but not of engineers). With these three conditions, potentially ambiguous information will be assimilated into the stereotype: we interpret the information in terms of the stereotype of the elderly person rather than, say, in terms of tiredness or injury, as in *the partygoer found it difficult to get up* or *the boxer found it difficult to get up*.

Interestingly, Stapel and Koomen (1998) argue that there is a case when priming a stereotype can result in the behaviour being interpreted in a less stereotypical way. This occurs when the ambiguous information about a person is primed by a relevant exemplar. In contrast with the unambiguously frail elderly person exemplar the ambiguous behaviour of the second person is viewed less stereotypically (as a result of the comparison process).

When do we use stereotypes to judge a person?

We saw in the previous chapter that impression formation is often a categorical judgement but this does not exclude the possibility that under certain circumstances we may judge a person on the specific individuating information we have about them (as Anderson, 1965, suggested). Fiske and her colleagues (Fiske *et al.*, 1987; Pavelchak, 1989) examined the circumstances in which a person makes a categorical judgement or an individuating judgement. In part one of a study by Fiske *et al.* (1987) participants rated the likeability of various category labels, such as *doctor*, *loan shark*. They also independently rated the likeability of sets of five traits (e.g. *curious, energetic, perceptive, aggressive, liberal*). Four weeks later, in the second part of the study, the participants were presented with a job category (e.g. *doctor*) and a set of five traits (e.g. *practical, educated, scientific, skilled, observant*). They had to rate the person on likeability, how typical this person was of the category, and how possible it was that a person in the category would have the traits listed. The researchers produced four conditions: consistent (where the traits were consistent with the stereotype of the category, such as the traits listed above with *doctor*); label-focus, where the traits listed with a category were uninformative (e.g. *adult, medium height*); inconsistent (where the traits from one category, such as the *artist* traits of *nonconforming, creative, eccentric, idealistic, fashionable*, were listed with a different category label, such as *hotel maid*); and attribute-focus, where the category label was uninformative (e.g. *person*).

A comparison between the ratings in the two parts of the study allowed the researchers to see whether the impressions of the category *plus* the trait set in part two were more like the category impressions *or* the trait set impressions of part one. In line with the hypotheses, the consistent and label-focus conditions led to more categorical impressions, and the inconsistent and attribute-focus conditions led to more trait-based impressions. Fiske *et al.* (1987) argued that in some circumstances we make categorical judgements of people. However, in other circumstances we make more individuating judgements based on the information we have about them. Fiske and Neuberg (1990) developed a model of impression formation that explained what circumstances would lead to which type of judgement.

According to the *continuum model of impression formation* (Fiske and Neuberg, 1990) we make an *initial categorization* of a person on the basis of the initial information we learn about them. This might well be on an obvious characteristic such as their age, gender or ethnicity. Fiske and Taylor (1991) suggest that this occurs automatically. If the person is of no interest (say, someone we are passing in the street) we will not bother to analyse them further. However, if we are motivated to consider the person further, we will then attend to the information about the person. For example, you are looking for a second-hand car and the salesman activates your stereotype of 'used-car dealer'. However, the car looks quite a good buy. Is he lying to you (consistent with your initial categorization) or is he offering a good deal? If additional information seems to fit your initial judgement then you have *category confirmation*. You are confirmed, in your view of the salesman and leave it at that. If, however, the category is not confirmed, then you engage in *recategorization*, and attempt to find a category that is a better fit – maybe the salesman is recategorized as a 'helpful assistant' or is seen to be like Tom, your father's friend, who sold cars honestly. If we cannot fit the person to a category then we engage in *piecemeal integration* of the information we have about them. There are also occasions when we are motivated to engage in piecemeal integration. Imagine you must choose between two candidates for a particularly important job. You are motivated to 'get it right' and may spend a lot of time and attention considering each of their attributes, attempting to develop an overall picture of them. Fiske and Neuberg (1990) argue that our impressions lie on a continuum from automatic initial categorizations to thoughtful piecemeal integration, dependent on how much time and attention we allocate to the information and the ease of fitting the person to a particular category.

Studies have shown that the amount of attention can influence whether the judgement is categorical or more individuated. Pratto and Bargh (1991) looked at the effect of attention on impression formation by presenting the information to the participants either briefly or more leisurely. When time was restricted the impression tended to be more stereotypical, despite the presence of inconsistent individuating information. In another study, Nelson et al. (1996) asked participants to decide whether a person description was of a nursing or an engineering student. The description, including a photograph of a man or a woman, included either typical male or female interests. Most descriptions also included individuating information about the person that would aid the judgement task, such as their hobbies and temporary jobs they had done. The researchers told some of the participants that the sex of the person was not helpful in judging their person's subject of study. They also told them that they would have to explain their decisions. Thus, the participants were motivated to pay attention to individuating information. Both these manipulations resulted in less stereotyping than for other participants, indicating that the participants could consciously influence the impression formed. However, the influence of the stereotypes did not disappear completely: the sex of a person still had an influence on a judgement.

Attention, memory and stereotypes

When we recall information about a person, what do we remember? Having categorized a person as, say, an *extrovert*, then it is likely that we will remember information consistent with the category: they were *outgoing* and *gregarious*. We may even recall that they were *outgoing* even though we did not explicitly receive this information (Cantor and Mischel, 1977). Stereotypes not only favour the encoding and representation of consistent information (Macrae *et al.*, 1994) but stereotype-consistent information is often better recalled, particularly when we are cognitively 'busy' (Macrae *et al.*, 1993). In recalling a person we briefly saw and categorized as an extrovert we might well recall they were talkative.

But this does not mean that stereotype-inconsistent information is poorly recalled. Hastie and Kumar (1979) presented a trait list to participants to give the impression of an 'intelligent person'. They then gave the participants descriptions of the behaviour of the person which were consistent (*won the chess tournament*), neutral (*took the lift to the third floor*) and inconsistent (*made the same mistake three times*) with the impression. Memory for the inconsistent behaviours was good, particularly when there were only a few of them compared to consistent behaviours. The good recall of inconsistent information may result from paying more attention to it (Hastie, 1981). We do not need to explain why an intelligent person won a chess tournament or did well in an examination, as it fits into our stereotype of intelligent person. However, we need to think about why an intelligent person made the same mistake three times, as it does not fit the stereotype and so we attend to it more. Inconsistent information requires attention to understand it. As we saw above, it may mean that we question our initial categorization of the person.

What happens when we are unable to attend to inconsistent information due to distraction or cognitive 'load'? Dijksterhuis and van Knippenberg (1995) presented information at different speeds, and Macrae *et al.*'s (1993) participants were required to remember an eight-digit number. When information was presented quickly in the former study stereotype-consistent information was recalled better than inconsistent information, and the cognitively 'busy' participants in the latter study also favoured consistent information in recall. Sherman *et al.* (1998) argue that we need to be careful in interpreting how stereotypes operate. It may be too rigid to view the 'busy' person as being unable to deal with inconsistent information. It may well be that stereotypes allow us to deal with consistent information efficiently when 'busy', but this efficiency of processing frees up attention which can then be used to deal with inconsistent or novel information.

According to this model, stereotypes do not merely simplify information processing for lazy perceivers with limited capacity [the 'cognitive miser' idea]; they also permit the flexible distribution of encoding resources in a way that maximizes the amount of information gained for the effort expended.

(Sherman *et al.*, 1998, p. 591)

Consider the following information: a man works as an engineer, likes making detailed models of sailing ships, does not like abstract art, likes logic puzzles, is not interested in politics and is a highly effective public speaker. Having categorized him as an engineer our stereotype of engineer leads us to process the consistent information about him very efficiently. However, we do not stereotypically associate engineers with effective public speaking. Thus, we can focus our attention on this piece of inconsistent information. We have 'freed up our mind' to concentrate on this. Why is he different in this way? How do we explain this? Is our initial categorization correct? If so, what is it about him that has led to this quality? Did he have special training? Concentrating on this inconsistent information may lead us to develop a more complex impression of the man.

Summary

There is evidence to suggest that there are two modes of human mental processing: first, conscious attention that takes time and effort but can operate flexibly, systematically and logically; and, second, automatic processing that is fast and relies on practised responses or heuristics but is inflexible. Heuristic thinking may result in a pragmatic solution to many problems but can also result in illusory correlations and illogical or non-probabilistic reasoning. Stereotypes can be considered as a form of heuristic thinking as they are processed quickly and efficiently and may be activated automatically. However, people may not be viewed stereotypically if the perceiver is motivated to pay attention to individuating information such as information that is inconsistent with the activated stereotype.

Further reading

Chaiken, S. and Trope, Y. (eds) (1999) *Dual-process theories in social psychology*. New York: Guilford Press. A review of the range of dual-process theories in social psychology.

Fiske, S.T. and Taylor, S.E. (1991) *Social cognition*. 2nd edition. New York: McGraw-Hill.

Robertson, S.I. (1999) *Types of thinking*. London: Routledge. A readable account of the cognitive studies of human thinking and problem solving.

Spears, R. and Haslam, S.A. (1997) 'Stereotyping and the burden of cognitive load', in R. Spears, P.J. Oakes, N. Ellemers and S.A. Haslam (eds) *The social psychology of stereotyping and group life*. Oxford: Blackwell. Considers stereotyping when called upon to perform other cognitive tasks simultaneously.

Chapter 4

Stereotypes as explanations: attribution and inference

Introduction

E XPLAINING WHY PEOPLE behave as they do is a key problem for the social perceiver and in this chapter we shall be considering the influence of stereotypes in explanations. Why did John hit Brian? Why did your date fail to turn up? Why did Susan pass the examination despite spending little time revising? When faced with these sorts of questions the social perceiver might attempt a thoughtful consideration of the situation. Is John known for hitting people? Did Brian provoke him? Was it a playful push rather than a hit? Finding the answers to these questions might lead to a reasoned answer to why John hit Brian. But as we saw in Chapter 3 human thinking is not always thought out in this careful way. We might decide heuristically that John, with his skinhead haircut, is a thug, or that Brian, known as a practical joker, has upset the wrong person. Notice that in applying the 'skinhead' stereotype to John we are using the stereotype to explain the action. Stereotypically skinheads are violent and John is a skinhead so that is why John acted in that way. We can see here that in applying a stereotype we are also providing an explanation for the event, so stereotypes can be viewed as explanations of social activity (Yzerbyt *et al.*, 1997).

Snap judgements

Snap judgements save us much effortful and time-consuming thought. Once we have categorized a person we can then 'explain' them stereotypically. Television situation comedies often present characters in stereotypical ways – the layabout son, the fussy grandma and so on – and much of the comedy relies on us making inferences from these stereotypes: the layabout son's room is a mess (as we expect) but why is he making grandma a meal (unexpected)? Has he got an ulterior motive? Does he want to borrow money to go out? Stereotypes provide us with a ready explanation of a person's behaviour when it is expected. It is unexpected behaviour that is more difficult to explain and that is where the comedy often lies. Politicians may exploit our snap judgements – if they dress smartly and speak confidently then we may well categorize them as trustworthy rather than incompetent. We saw in Chapter 3 that when not paying attention we may well be persuaded by 'peripheral cues' that activate stereotypical explanations.

When we observe other people we do not simply gain an impression about them, we use that impression to explain their behaviour. For example, on encountering the aftermath of a car crash we might seek out what happened. Fortunately no one is hurt but there is damage to the two cars involved. A young man is the driver of a new red sports car and an elderly woman is the driver of an older small car. What do we conclude? Do we conclude that the young man was driving too fast or that the old woman did not see the other car? If so, it is our stereotypes of the two ages that are guiding our judgement. But surely this is a serious incident where we would be more measured in our judgement and not jump to conclusions? Maybe the accident report will show that the woman was driving too fast or that the man was not paying attention. In many cases the judgement made will have serious consequences for the people involved, such as with a defendant in a court case when the jurors must decide who is telling the truth. Yet do we weigh the evidence or employ stereotypical judgements of the defendant according to the way they look and act: he looks a nasty piece of work; she looks too meek to have committed such a crime?

83

Considered judgements: attribution theory

When we decide why someone did something we are making an *attribution* of a cause to an effect. I believe that Susan lent me some money because she likes me but the politician chatted to me in the street because he wants my vote rather than because he likes me. It was Heider (1958) who first considered in detail the attributions people make about the behaviour of others. Notice here that we are not considering the actual reasons for behaviour (if it were possible to discover them) but the reasons people give for the behaviour of others. Heider argued that we wish to understand the world in order to predict and control it. In explaining the behaviour of others he suggested that we are like 'naive scientists' seeking evidence for the causes of behaviour. He suggested that we wish to make a distinction between *intentional* behaviour and *accidental* behaviour. If we decide that a person pushed us by accident (they slipped and pushed us as they fell) then we will act differently to if we decide it was deliberate (they are a bully or they were in a rush to get past). Interestingly, Heider (1958) argued that as behaviour is more salient than environmental factors we are often biased in favour of personal causation. In a car accident we may infer it is one of the drivers' fault, ignoring the mechanics of the car or the weather conditions.

Jones and Davis (1965) developed Heider's ideas in their work. Their particular focus was on the conditions that lead to a *correspondent inference*, that is, when do we infer that behaviour arises out of the characteristics of the person, such as: John refused to lend me some money because he is *mean*. To make a correspondent inference we must analyse certain aspects of the situation, to infer the intention of the person. First, we must decide that the behaviour was *freely chosen* by the person. You might make a correspondent inference about someone who always chooses to go to bed at the same time, but not if they are in prison where they are required to go to bed at the same time each night. Second, we must decide that the person has the *ability* (and knowledge) to intentionally perform the behaviour. I will not assume that a 6-month-old baby who punches me on the nose intended it in the same way as an adult who does the same thing. Third, we must look at the effects of an action. The more common effects there are resulting from the action the harder it is to choose why someone did one thing and not the other, so we look for *noncommon effects*. Why did John choose to go to one university and not another? The universities may be equally prestigious, the courses equally good, the campuses equally pleasant. However, one is on the coast and the other is not. This is a noncommon effect. This will help us decide why John made his choice. We also consider the *desirability* of the effects. It is assumed that we all want desirable effects of our actions so if someone chooses to do something that has undesirable effects then we are more likely to make a correspondent inference: Jane spends all her time studying, or working to support her studies, and has no time for a social life, so we infer she really wants that degree. Finally, we are more likely to make a correspondent inference with out-of-role behaviour than in-role behaviour. In-role behaviour is expected and is a requirement of the role, so the caring nurse and helpful shop assistant are behaving in role. However, if a nurse behaves in an uncaring way we may well see this out-of-role behaviour as emanating from his or her character.

This process of deciding whether to make a correspondent inference or not involves quite a detailed analysis of the information available, where we act as the 'naive scientist' weighing up the information. However, Jones and McGillis (1976) modified the theory to include our expectations. Desirability of behaviour and in-role behaviour are really expectations based on our knowledge of people. So we will have expectations about how certain people will behave. Thus, stereotypes can be seen as category-based expectations: we expect young men to drive too fast; we expect older people to be slow. When a member of a stereotyped group does the unexpected then we may see it as arising from their individual character (that makes them an exception).

Kelley (1967) argued that the naive scientist is performing an analysis of the variation in different behaviours when making an attribution. This was termed the *covariation model*. When deciding whether a piece of behaviour was caused by the person or the situation, says Kelley, we examine the variation in three factors. We look at whether other people do the same in the same circumstances (*consensus*), we examine whether the behaviour is different to that performed by the same person in other circumstances (*distinctiveness*), and whether the person does the same thing in the same circumstances (*consistency*). McArthur (1972) tested Kelley's theory by giving participants questions such as *why did John laugh at the comedian?* – along with information about consensus, distinctiveness and consistency. Their attributions were as Kelley predicted. If consensus was low (*no one else laughed*), distinctiveness was low (*John laughs at other comedians*) and consistency was high (*John always laughs at this comedian*) then an attribution to the person was made (John is the sort of person who laughs at any comedian). If all three factors are high, then everyone laughs at this comedian, John doesn't laugh at other comedians, and has always laughed at this one: so the attribution of John's laughter is to the comedian who is very funny. McArthur's findings supported Kelley's theory.

However, Kelley (1973) acknowledged that this is a rather idealized view of the perceiver making attributions: we need to have the time and the information as well as the motivation to undertake this detailed analysis (which McArthur's participants had). In everyday experience we often do not have all the information (or the inclination) to perform the analysis. In this case, argues Kelley, we rely on causal schemas to make attributions. Causal schemas are our learnt expectations and assumptions about the relationships between causes and effects. As each action has many possible causes as well as many possible effects we use our knowledge to *discount* certain causes and *augment* other causes. If an actor gets paid a lot of money to endorse a product, we are likely to discount 'he did it because he really likes it' in favour of 'he did it for the money'. Similarly, if a person gives up their holiday to help refugees, then the fact that they have given up their holiday will augment the belief that they did it because they are a caring person. In these cases when we do not have much information about a person (or have not paid attention to it) our prior knowledge and expectations guide our attributions.

Attributional biases

Once again when considering cognition we are faced with the situation that we have evidence that people can reason out a solution to a problem given enough information and the knowledge, ability, time and inclination to use it (such as McArthur's (1972) findings). However, as we have seen in Chapter 3, it is often the case that people do not engage in a considered reasoning process but employ strategies: 'rules of thumb' or heuristics. In attribution research it has been shown that, compared to an outcome arising from logical or statistical principles, we are often biased in our attributions.

Certain biases may be due to the type of information available or the attention we pay to it. Following from Heider, it has been argued that people tend to attribute causes to the person rather than the situation, even when the person is constrained by circumstances in terms of what they can do. This is termed the *fundamental attribution error* (Ross, 1977). It is possible that greater attention is paid to the person rather than the situation. Gilbert *et al.* (1988) showed that someone who was 'cognitively busy' (see Chapter 3) made less use of situational information and made more attributions to the person. Interestingly, this does not occur when we attribute causes to our own actions. Whereas we will look at the person who drops a plate in a restaurant as clumsy (an attribution to the person), when *we* drop the plate we tend to make an attribution to the situation (the plate was slippery). This is called the *actor–observer effect* (Jones and Nisbett, 1971). Again, following Heider, it may be that the behaviour of other people is more salient than the situational factors, whereas for our own actions the situational factors are more salient. It may also be that we have more information about our own actions and thus consider the situational factors more with our own behaviour (Fiske and Taylor, 1991).

Other biases may arise from motivational reasons. People tend to attribute their successes to internal factors (*I passed that examination because I am clever*) and their failures to external factors (*I failed that examination because the questions were confusing*). This is termed the *self-serving bias* (Miller and Ross, 1975). The bias allows us to view ourselves positively (Reiss *et al.*, 1981). Self-serving biases might also be employed to maintain one's particular beliefs. Deaux (1976) noted that, in certain cases, success in men and women was attributed to different causes: in men it was seen as due to ability but in women it was attributed to luck or hard work. Why should a change in gender change the attribution? Rather than taking equal success as indicating equal ability, the answer appears to be that the attributions are based on the stereotype where women are seen as of lower ability than men. If a woman has to work harder than a man to achieve the same success then the stereotypical view can be maintained. Note here that we can argue that the explanation could be cognitive (an underlying stereotypical belief guides the attribution) or motivational (a desire to maintain a sexist view of the world). We can also see that evidence that would logically be seen as indicating that a stereotype is false can, by making specific attributions, be used to support the stereotyped view. These are very important points in stereotype research which we will take up in a consideration of Billig's work in Chapter 6.

A related bias is the *false consensus effect* (Ross *et al.*, 1977). This is the belief that most other people would act as we do. Ross *et al.* (1977) asked students if they would carry a sandwich board with 'Eat at Joe's' written on it. The people who said 'yes' predicted that 62 per cent of students would do the same, and the people who said 'no' predicted that 67 per cent of students would do the same as them. Assuming that others will act like us saves us the effort of seeking out actual consensus information and also allows us to maintain the view that we are typical or 'normal' people.

We may make attributions that make it appear that bad things are not likely to occur to us: defensive attributions (Shaver, 1970). Lerner (1980) argued that certain people may hold a belief that the world is fair and just: good things happen to good people and bad things happen to bad people. This is termed the *Just World Hypothesis*. If we hold this belief, then, seeing ourself as a good person, we can believe that bad things won't happen to us. It is a self-serving bias. However, what happens when we find out that something bad has happened to a good person? Rather than changing our view of the world we may do three things to retain our belief (Lerner and Miller, 1978):

1   Compensate the victim. For example, if a young child has a favourite bike stolen we might club together to buy them a new one 'to restore the child's faith in others'.
2   Blame the victim. For example, the mugging victim is viewed as being partly responsible for the attack by taking a shortcut through an alleyway which 'everyone knew' to be a dangerous thing to do.
3   Derogate the victim. For example, a rape victim's past sexual behaviour is used to imply she was promiscuous.

A number of other attributional biases have been examined. For example, there is a *hindsight bias* or the 'knew-it-all-along' effect (Roese and Olson, 1996) where people claim after an event that they predicted the outcome that occurred. For example, after a man is found guilty of a murder a person claims that they knew he was guilty all along yet prior to the verdict they had not asserted any confidence in the man's guilt. It may be that the hindsight bias helps people to make sense of unexpected outcomes (Roese and Olson, 1996): when the mild-mannered family man from down the street turns out to be a serial killer the world seems a more predictable place if you decide: *I knew something was strange about that guy.*

What do all these biases add up to? Roese and Olson (1996) provide an answer: 'The hindsight bias is best viewed on the same conceptual playing field as other functionally sound cognitive simplifications, such as attitudes, stereotypes, and impressions: Quick and often pragmatically useful inferences that are some-times made at the expense of accuracy' (p. 224). As we have seen in Chapter 3, much of human thinking involves using heuristics rather than engaging in more considered time-consuming thought. It appears that this is also the case with attributions (Fiske and Taylor, 1991), in that often we do not seek out the logical or statistically appropriate explanation but rely on our expectations and assumptions about what causes people to behave as they do. Indeed, as has been pointed out (Semin and Manstead, 1983), we do not need to explain expected behaviour as it fits in with what we believe to be the case: the introvert quietly reading a book, the engineer making detailed models for a hobby. It is only unexpected behaviour that might make us stop and think what could have caused it.

Stereotypes and attributions

Whilst attribution theory presents the person as trying to work out a cause for an effect and the biases show that we do not always do this logically or statistically, there are many cases where we do not work out an explanation. Why did John hit Brian *in the boxing ring*? Why did Peter kick the ball *in the soccer match?* Because that is the point of the sport! As Semin (1980) points out, we do not need to explain behaviour that follows social convention. The fact that Susan shakes David's hand when they meet or Paul orders a drink in a bar is hardly surprising as that is what people do when they meet or when they go into a bar in our *culture*. It appears so obvious that it apparently requires no explanation. Often it is only when we meet a person from a different culture that we suddenly become aware that the social conventions of our culture are not universal.

We can consider stereotypes as being like social conventions (see Chapter 7). Stereotypes provide us with ready explanations. When people follow stereotypical expectations, such as an Italian looking chic or a Frenchman drinking wine, the explanation is contained within the stereotype. When using a stereotype we are making an attribution: we attribute the assumed group characteristics to the person being stereotyped. This person is English so will be tradition-loving, this person is Brazilian so will have a sense of rhythm. We can then make further attributions based on the stereotype. Why is the Englishman drinking tea at 4 o'clock in the afternoon? Because it is traditional for people to have afternoon tea in England. That is what Englishmen do: it is what they are like, it is in their nature. Stereotypes are essentially internal attributions. When we attribute the stereotypical characteristic of *caring* to a doctor, *ambitious* to a lawyer or *boring* to an accountant we are not saying that the situation is determining their actions, but an internal disposition.

These internal attributions can be seen as representing the fundamental attribution error: we are overestimating internal causation. It is the role of doctors and nurses to care for the sick, so when we attribute their care to a *caring nature* we may be ignoring the requirements of the role. Doctors are required to be caring by their role and can be barred from practising if they are not. As we shall see below (under self-fulfilling prophesies), we may even attribute the act of an uncaring doctor, who hurts us more than necessary when giving an injection, to situational factors, such as the pain of the needle – thus maintaining our view that doctors are caring.

Stereotypes can also be seen as providing a rationalization for social divisions (Yzerbyt *et al.*, 1997; see also Chapter 6). Why are some people poor and some people rich? If we attribute stereotypical personality characteristics such as *lazy* and *unintelligent* to the poor people and *hard-working* and *intelligent* to the rich, then when we 'explain' why one group is poor and one rich we can attribute it to their nature rather than discrimination in the social conditions. Thus, stereotypes provide a justification of the status quo. In a study by Hoffman and Hurst (1990) participants were presented with descriptions of people belonging to one of two groups on a distant planet, Orinthians and Ackmians. They were also told that there was only one sex on the planet, so anyone could mate with anyone else and all people could reproduce. However, Orinthians were described predominantly as *city workers* and Ackmians were predominantly *child raisers*. Not only did stereotypes of the groups emerge, analogous to male and female stereotypes, but, when participants were asked to explain why there was the association between the groups and the roles, the attributions were to personality characteristics, implying a rationalization of the social division.

Stereotypical expectations

Just as we do not need to explain why the players kick the ball in a soccer match, as that is what we expect them to do, stereotypes also provide us with a set of expectations that explain behaviour. Even for people we have encountered only briefly there are 'automatic' explanations available by which to interpret their actions. Consider the basic physical characteristics we detect on seeing someone for the first time. First, we can see their age, gender and ethnicity and so immediately place them into a sub-category of persons: Hispanic boy, young white woman, elderly black man (Fiske, 1992b). Each of these can be used to activate a stereotype. Ethnic stereotyping has been studied most in psychological research, with gender stereotyping next and age stereotyping rather less. It is clear from Katz and Braly (1933) onwards that there are commonly known stereotypes of ethnic groups, with characteristics such as *intelligence* stereotypically associated with Asians and *athleticism* stereotypically associated with blacks (e.g. Stangor and Lange, 1994). Gender stereotypes appear to be related to the traditional social roles that men and women inhabit (Eagly and Steffen, 1984), so women are stereotypically more *caring* than men and men are stereotypically more *aggressive* than women. The research on age stereotypes has looked primarily at the elderly stereotype, with characteristics such as *lonely* and *forgetful* stereotypically attributed to old age (e.g. Bargh *et al.*, 1996). Notice how these stereotypes are linked to physical characteristics which we as individuals have little control over. Whereas we can choose our occupation we cannot choose our gender. Thus, the woman doctor may be stereotypically attributed the characteristics of *caring* for her *achieved role* of doctor (a role she achieved through her own actions) or for her *ascribed role* of woman (the sex-role of a woman is ascribed to her by society) (Fiske and Taylor, 1991).

A number of other physical features can be used to stereotype. Jackson and Ervin (1992) showed that short men and women were perceived less favourably than their taller counterparts, with shorter people perceived as having a lower professional status. Ryckman *et al.* (1989) found that there were stereotypes of body shape, with people of athletic build seen as more *hard-working* than those with a fatter, rounded form, and with thinner people viewed as *intelligent* and *neat*. Berry and McArthur (1986) found that adults with facial immaturity ('babyfacedness') were perceived as *warmer* but *weaker* than adults with more mature-looking faces. Physical attractiveness has been shown to lead to a number of advantages for the attractive individual (Berscheid, 1985), arising from the stereotype termed 'what is beautiful is good' by Dion *et al.* (1972). For example, a bad essay was given a better mark when the marker believed the writer was attractive (Landy and Sigall, 1974), and an attractive defendant was given a more lenient sentence for certain crimes in a study by Sigall and Ostrove (1975).

Hair styles and hair colour, spectacles, clothes and jewellery can all provide information that can lead to a stereotypical attribution of personality characteristics (see Hinton, 1993). So, even before a person actually does something, a perceiver will have expectations about them. We can see these stereotypical explanations operating in a number of studies on jury decision making.

Stereotypical explanations and jury attributions

A juror is placed in a difficult position. It is a new experience, unlike any other, and they are called upon to make a reasoned decision based on the evidence presented in court. Occasionally someone will say something in court that the jurors are told to ignore, which they may not be able to do. But most of the time they will have to decide who is telling the truth and decide upon the guilt or innocence of a defendant. How do they do this? To try to understand the processes involved in jury decision making psychologists have presented either a group of people or individuals with brief accounts of a crime and asked them to make a decision.

The results of mock jury studies have supported the view that our decisions (attributions of guilt) are influenced by stereotypes. Consider how you imagine someone guilty of grievous bodily harm looks (or a drug pusher or a fraudster). If the defendant in the dock looks like your stereotype of such a criminal, will it affect your judgement? Research by Macrae and Shepherd (1989) has shown that it does. Raters judged photographs of male faces on honesty and aggressiveness to produce a set of faces that ranged in honesty and a set that ranged in aggressiveness. From the honesty set different raters picked the faces most and least likely to commit a theft, and from the aggressive set they picked the faces most and least likely to commit an assault. Finally participants viewed one of the faces whilst listening to a description of a crime the person had been accused of. The man with a dishonest face was seen as guilty of the crime by significantly more participants than the man with the honest face. Similarly the aggressive-faced man was judged to be guilty of assault by more participants than the man with the less aggressive-looking face.

The pervasive effect of stereotypes was shown in a study by Bodenhausen (1990). As expected, a person who was accused of a stereotypical crime (in this case a Hispanic accused of assault) was seen as more likely to really be guilty than a nonstereotypical defendant. Interestingly, when a not-guilty verdict was included in the information, the participants' judgement showed a hindsight bias with a nonstereotypical defendant. The judgement of innocence rose significantly: *I knew he was innocent all along.* However, with stereotypical crimes the not-guilty verdict did not affect the participants' judgement of guilt. The person was viewed as just as likely to be guilty as when no verdict was given. There was no *I knew he was innocent* hindsight bias but a stereotypical: *I think he's just as likely to be guilty despite the verdict.*

Research has shown that a range of stereotypes influence judgements. For example, attractive people are assumed to be good (the *what is beautiful is good* stereotype) so they are given the 'benefit of the doubt' when they do wrong. For example, an attractive woman convicted of burglary was given a shorter sentence than a less attractive woman (Sigall and Ostrove, 1975), and an attractive victim leads to greater severity from a jury (Kerr, 1978).

We do need to be careful when we assess the effects of stereotypes on jury decisions. Many of the studies provide the mock jurors with very little information about the legal case. If participants only have a brief description, then maybe we should not be surprised if a face or name stereotype influences their judgement: it may be all they have to go on. When more detailed information is provided the stereotype does not always affect the judgement (Jones, 1997).

Stereotypes and expectancy

Stereotypes provide us with an interpretative framework by which we can explain the behaviour of others. We hardly need to ask: why did the doctor save the dying child? It is what we expect doctors to do. It is more difficult to explain the opposite: why did the doctor leave the child to die?

Much of what happens in our daily lives is expected. We saw in Chapter 2 that Kelly (1955) argued that we learn to predict people and events so that we can make sense of what is happening in the social world around us. We not only learn that restaurants serve meals, that badminton is played with a shuttlecock and that football is a game of two halves, but we also learn that lawyers are intelligent and well-dressed and librarians are quiet and responsible. But what happens when we encounter the unambitious lawyer or the irresponsible librarian? An important finding is that we spend more time considering the unexpected information than the expected information (see Chapter 3; also Lalonde and Gardner, 1989; Johnson and Hewstone, 1992). The key question is: what is the result of the extra consideration of the unexpected information? Later in the chapter we will be considering how counter-stereotypical information influences our stereotypes. Here we are interested in how unexpected information influences our judgement of a person.

Expectancy violation and evaluation

When people violate our stereotypical expectancies, such as a politician telling the truth or a computer programmer winning a weight-lifting contest, then according to *expectancy violation theory* we evaluate them more extremely than other people who do the same things or have the same characteristics (Jussim *et al.*, 1987). Thus, the priest who steals from an old lady will be viewed more negatively than the petty crook who does the same. It may be that unexpected behaviour requires us to pay attention or that unexpected information is more diagnostic about what a person is like. However, Jussim *et al.* (1987) draw on Kelley's principles of discounting and augmenting to explain the expectancy violation effect. Compare two people who achieve the same high political office: one is a rich white man who went to all the best schools, and the other a poor black woman who is self-educated. How do we rate the personality characteristics of these two people? Who is more intelligent, stronger-willed and determined? The presence of other causal factors, such as wealth and education, will discount the personal characteristics of the white man, whereas the obstacles, such as racial prejudice and poverty, will augment the qualities of the black woman and she will be seen more positively.

In a study examining expectancy-violation Jussim *et al.* (1987) asked participants to evaluate candidates who were supposedly photographed and recorded during a job interview (but the materials were actually produced by the experimenters). The job candidates were either a black or a white man, upper- or lower-class, and spoke in standard or nonstandard English. It was assumed that for the white participants in the study the upper-class, standard-speaking black man violated their stereotypical expectancies. In line with the prediction this candidate was rated higher than an upper-class, standard-speaking white man on a number of characteristics such as likelihood of being hired, intelligence and competence.

Expectancy violation was not able to explain all the results in Jussim *et al.*'s study and they suggested that the concepts of *complexity–extremity theory* (Linville and Jones, 1980) and *assumed characteristics theory* may be involved as well. The former theory suggests that we are more cognitively complex (see Chapter 2) in our evaluation of members of our own social group than with members of other groups. When we judge someone from our own group on a number of dimensions the overall evaluation tends to be less extreme as there will be a mixture of positive and negative judgements. When judging someone from another social group on only a few dimensions there is a greater chance of an extreme judgement. The latter theory – assumed characteristics theory – proposes that direct knowledge of people's characteristics (upper-class, standard English speaker) will have more impact on the person doing the judging than group membership (black or white) so will reduce outgroup negativity.

Bettencourt *et al.* (1997) asked white subjects to give an expectancy rating of job candidates. They showed that, in line with the stereotypes, participants rated the skilled black candidate and unskilled white candidate as unexpected. Furthermore the evaluation of the candidates showed that the skilled black candidate was rated higher than the skilled white candidate, and the unskilled white candidate was rated lower than the unskilled black candidate, as predicted by expectancy violation theory. Bettencourt *et al.* also found a similar pattern of results when the job candidates were male or female for a stereotypically male job (sports writer) and stereotypically female job (fashion writer). As the researchers point out, when we are aware that a person's behaviour violates our stereotypical expectation of them (as a member of the stereotyped group) it has an important effect on our overall evaluation of them.

The resistance of stereotypes to change

If we view people as being able to develop and change their ideas when encountering new information, then stereotypes should change. A common theme in social psychology, proposed by authors such as Heider (1958), Kelly (1955) and Kelley (1973), is that we act like scientists in attempting to find the best explanation to fit the information available. Therefore, when encountering information inconsistent with a stereotype we should change the stereotypical explanation to better fit the evidence. Unfortunately, this appears to depend very much on the circumstances. In a number of situations the presence of counter-stereotypical information may not be enough for a re-evaluation of the belief. The following sections will consider explanations of why this might be.

The self-confirming nature of stereotypes

Imagine that you are a teacher and you hold a negative stereotypical view that members of a particular ethnic group are not very intelligent. Does your experience of teaching members of this group lead to you changing your views when you find that they are as intelligent as other groups? The answer is possibly not. Believing a child from the group to be less intelligent than the others you may act differently towards the child, giving them less attention and assistance than others, in the belief that it will not help them. The intelligent child, perceiving your disinterest, may become disillusioned with the work and perform below their potential. You then see the child's performance and see that it is worse than that of children from other ethnic groups – and apparently your stereotyped view is confirmed! This is termed a *self-fulfilling prophesy* (Snyder *et al.*, 1977): a person acts in a way that brings about the stereotypical outcome they believe to be the case.

Snyder *et al.* (1977) examined the *what is beautiful is good* stereotype in their own study. Male and female students spoke over the telephone but could not see each other. Male participants were led to believe that their partner was either physically attractive or unattractive. Surprisingly, the female conversationalist appeared friendlier and more sociable if her male partner believed her to be attractive, regardless of her true level of physical attractiveness. The authors argued that the male participants, expecting the attractive women to be nicer, adjusted their way of interacting with her to bring this about.

However, we should not overestimate the size of this effect. Recent work has indicated that it may not be very large in practice (e.g. Jussim *et al.*, 1996). For example, Smith *et al.* (1998) examined the mathematical performance of 1,701 sixth-grade schoolchildren against teacher perceptions of the children's abilities. Some evidence was found for a self-fulfilling prophesy with respect to the lower-ability children. It was suggested that the teachers assessed lower-ability children less accurately than the higher-ability children possibly as a result of spending less time with the lower-ability children. However, Smith *et al.* argued that the self-fulfilling prophesy was a relatively small effect and that the teachers were generally quite accurate in their judgement of the children.

Stereotype preservation biases in information processing

The way we select and recall information about a person might also lead to the presence of inconsistent information failing to lead to stereotype change. The scientific way of testing our beliefs is to try to falsify them. If I believe that *all* Frenchmen make good chefs all I need to do is find one who is not and this will disprove my hypothesis. Interestingly, it appears that we may seek out confirming information rather than disconfirming information when attempting to test our beliefs (Snyder *et al.*, 1982; Johnson, 1996). Thus, rather than seeking out the Frenchman who is an awful cook, people will tend to look for more examples of successful French chefs. In this way the stereotype is preserved, as a long list of French chefs is produced in support of the original belief.

We may also be biased in our memory of information about a person when we stereotype them (van Knippenberg and Dijksterhuis, 1996). If you are told that John likes painting, enjoys logic puzzles, wears flamboyant clothes and likes gardening, and then you learn that he is an arts student, this may lead you to recall that he likes painting and wears flamboyant clothes better than that he likes logic puzzles and gardening. Van Knippenberg and Dijksterhuis suggest that the poorer recall of the stereotype-inconsistent information may help to preserve the stereotype. John is remembered as more consistent with the arts student stereotype by a memory bias against stereotype-inconsistent information.

Stereotype change

Stereotype change and subtyping

Given that stereotypes appear to be resistant to change it is important to know which circumstances do result in a change to a stereotype. In a key study Weber and Crocker (1983) presented participants with information about librarians, stereotypically seen as neat, quiet and responsible, and corporate lawyers, stereotypically viewed as well-dressed, industrious and intelligent. The information was about either six or thirty members of the group, with the counter-stereotypical information either concentrated in a few members or spread out throughout the group. When the counter-stereotypical information was concentrated in a few individuals or in highly unstereotypical instances, then subtyping occurred rather than stereotype change. This implied that an example such as Margaret Thatcher becoming the first woman Prime Minister of the United Kingdom in 1979 would not have led to a change to a stereotypical view of women being unable to wield political power effectively, due to her being subtyped as 'different' from 'normal' women (indicated by nicknames such as the 'iron lady' in references to her in the press). However, when the counter-stereotypical information was dispersed within the group, particularly when the group was large, stereotype change did occur. So the presence of over one hundred women Members of Parliament in the Government party following the United Kingdom election of 1997 should lead to greater stereotype change than was the case with the single distinctive example, since the politically powerful woman can no longer be perceived as a subtype.

Johnson and Hewstone (1992) also showed that counter-stereotypical information concentrated in a few individuals led to subtyping. They further showed that group members with counter-stereotypical information (e.g. a physics student who was fashion-conscious) were regarded as more typical of the group when the counter-stereotypical information was dispersed (each member was mostly stereotypical) than when the counter-stereotypical information was concentrated in a few individuals.

When members are seen as not typical of the group then they are subtyped. The participants took longer looking at the information of group members with some counter-stereotypical information in the dispersed condition. It was as though they were trying to make sense of the unexpected information concerning a group member, for example, *why is this typical physics student fashion-conscious?*

As Hewstone *et al.* (1994) explain, subtyping is a cognitive process that allows a perceiver to maintain a particular stereotypical view of a social group despite the acquisition of disconfirming information. Over time different subtypes may be formed subordinate to the overall category. For example, a man who holds a stereotypical view of women as *only* carers and homemakers will not change his view of women when faced with examples of successful business women (such as Anita Roddick of the Body Shop) but subtype them as a particular subset of women. Similarly, successful politicians who are women (such as Margaret Thatcher) will be subtyped rather than altering the overall view of women in general.

The generation of subtypes does have the effect of differentiating the group so that it can no longer be seen as composed of similar individuals. However, it may be that, in subtyping, a person is able to maintain, and even strengthen, their original stereotype of the group (with the exceptions of the subtypes) in the face of disconfirming information (Hewstone *et al.*, 1994). Kunda and Oleson (1995) argued that if a person can justify a subtype they will not change their stereotype despite the counter-evidence. In their study participants read an interview with a lawyer, Steve. The counter-stereotypical information was that Steve was introverted. Some participants read the additional neutral information that he worked for a small firm, and some were not given this information. The results indicated that the participants used the neutral information to justify maintaining their stereotype that lawyers are extroverted. If 'small firm lawyers' are subtyped as more introverted than other lawyers then the counter-stereotypical information is explained away rather than leading to a change in the stereotype.

Interestingly, Kunda and Oleson (1997) showed that an extremely counter-stereotypical example can lead to a boomerang effect: rather than changing the stereotype it leads to it being strengthened. In their study participants rated a public relations (PR) agent on extroversion (a stereotypical characteristic) before and after reading a description of an extremely introverted PR agent. For participants who viewed PR agents as moderately extroverted the exceptional case led to little change in their ratings. However, for participants who believed that PR agents were very extroverted a boomerang effect occurred: they rated PR agents as even more extroverted after reading the counter-example. The authors suggest that these participants reject the example if it can be seen as not typical of the category. So it is quite possible that sexists observing Margaret Thatcher as the first British woman Prime Minister, perceiving her to be atypical of women, may even have become more convinced of their stereotype of women in general.

The contact hypothesis

If stereotypes are inaccurate and people from one social group do not have much contact with the social group they view in a stereotypical way, then the stereotype is unlikely to change. However, if we can bring the two social groups together in a positive way, then, according to the *contact hypothesis* (Allport, 1954), the first group will view the second more accurately and stereotype change will occur.

Unfortunately, according to Hewstone and Brown (1986), stereotype change will only occur if the first group views the members of the second group whom they come into contact with as *typical* of their group. Otherwise, in line with the Weber and Crocker (1983) findings, the members of the second group may be subtyped as exceptions and the original stereotype is maintained despite the contact. In a test of this, Hewstone *et al.* (1992) looked at the views of 14–16-year-old schoolchildren concerning the police (in general) and the school police officer (whom they came into contact with through school–police liaison). Despite the children viewing the school police officer more positively than the police in general, contact with him did not result in an improvement in the children's view of the police when tested a year later. The results showed that the school police officer was not seen as typical of the police and was seen as engaging in different activities to other police officers. Thus, the contact with the school police officer did little to change the view of police in general.

Summary

When we endeavour to explain why a person acted as they did we may spend time and effort attempting to work out a reason for their behaviour. Attribution theory has offered models of how we do this. However, there is evidence that we make attributions of causes to behaviours heuristically, and stereotypes can be seen as heuristic explanations which, like social conventions, provide us with 'ready made' answers as to why people behave as they do. If people behave in a manner consistent with their stereotype then there appears to be no need for explanation. However, inconsistent behaviour may not lead to stereotype change for a number of reasons, one being that inconsistent individuals may be subtyped whilst the original stereotype is retained for the group *in general*. Stereotype change is most likely to occur when inconsistent behaviour is dispersed throughout the group.

Further reading

Brunas-Wagstaff, J. (1998) *Personality: a cognitive approach*. London: Routledge. Chapter 6 provides a brief summary of social decision making.

Fiske, S.T. and Taylor, S.E. (1991) *Social cognition*. 2nd edition. New York: McGraw-Hill. Chapter 2 is a review of the basic findings of attribution theory.

Yzerbyt, V., Rocher, S. and Schadron, G. (1997) 'Stereotypes as explanations: a subjective essentialistic view of group perception', in R. Spears, P. J. Oakes, N. Ellemers and S.A. Haslam (eds.) *The social psychology of stereotyping and group life.* Oxford: Blackwell. An interesting paper which considers stereotypes as providing perceivers with ways of making sense of social life – as providing explanations for actions and positions of social groups.

Chapter 5

Stereotyping and intergroup perception

Introduction: social groups

IT IS IMPORTANT TO APPRECIATE that stereotyping is not just an individual process. There is a temptation, in looking at cognitive processing to concentrate on individual cognition but we must not forget that stereotyping is fundamentally a group process. In categorizing a person we are invariably assigning them to a group. When we perceive someone as a friend we are viewing them as a member of the group of people we label 'friends' and not as part of another group, the people who are not our friends. Furthermore many categorizations assign people to a group that we are members of ourselves. At university we might perceive someone as a fellow psychology student rather than a student of history or physics. On the way to a sports event we recognize supporters of our team by their scarves and other insignia. In this chapter we shall look at how our own group membership influences our social judgements. This is the difference between categorizing objects (such as tables and chairs) and categorizing people (fellow countrymen and -women, foreigners). In categorizing someone as of the same nationality as myself I may also view them more positively than I view foreigners. Notice how the attribution to such a group has certain connotations. A person who is not from our country can be labelled an alien, a stranger, un étranger, an outlander, ein ausländer (Tajfel, 1978a). Social groups serve, as we shall see below, the key role of providing us with a *social identity* – a sense of who we are. This will also influence how we view other groups.

When we see categorization as a group definition we are then able to distinguish between two types of group: the *ingroup* of which the perceiver is a member, and an *outgroup* to which the perceiver does not belong. As the categorization arises on the basis of a key characteristic, such as nationality for the group 'British', the groups are distinguished in the research by the defining characteristic. If the ingroup is British then an outgroup will be another nationality, such as French, as that is the characteristic on which the groups are distinguished, but outgroups will not be defined on other characteristics (such as astronomers or children).

The salience of a group

Clearly, the categories we assign people to at any one time depend on the context in which we are experiencing them. On campus we may not use the group definition 'a member of the university' as almost all people are; we are more likely to distinguish between relevant or *salient* categories, such as fellow psychology students and students on other courses, or members of the orienteering club or rock-and-roll society of which we are a member. A category will be salient to the context in which the person is perceived (Fiske and Taylor, 1991). So, if the categorization into university membership or not becomes salient – for example, in checking identification to see who has access to certain buildings such as the library – then 'member of the university' may well be the group considered. It appears that *distinctiveness* may also lead to a person being categorized according to the distinctive characteristic. The one woman in a room of men is distinctive on gender and so gender may become a salient characteristic to a perceiver (Taylor *et al.*, 1978). Arguably, when we have little or no information about people we often draw on physical characteristics such as age, gender or ethnicity as the basis for social groupings, as they are immediately apparent in many instances. Furthermore, they are given a significance within our culture. Also, Oakes *et al.* (1991) showed that categories are salient when the category members act in accordance with the stereotype of them. Participants in one study saw on video a discussion between arts and science students. They employed the category membership to explain a student's comments (rather than the individual's personality) when the students in the discussion expressed views stereotypical of arts and science students.

Intergroup perception

Studies of prejudice in the mid-twentieth century had shown that it is basically an intergroup process (see Chapter 1). Dollard *et al.* (1939) had argued that frustration led to aggression towards certain social groups. In Adorno *et al.*'s (1950) research the authoritarian person directed their antagonism towards groups such as blacks or Jews. Sherif *et al.* (1961) had shown that intergroup hostility emerged with intergroup competition. The reasons prejudice arose were seen as primarily due to motivational, emotional and evolutionary factors. However, an important shift occurred with the work of Tajfel and his colleagues on intergroup perception. Tajfel (1969) argued that the cognitive processes in categorization were also involved in prejudice. He criticized the prevailing view of prejudice that ignored cognition:

> When we think of human attempts to understand the physical or the biological environment, man appears essentially as an exploring and rational animal . . . however imperfect the exploring rationality appears to be. But there seems to be one exception to this model . . . The prevailing model of man as a creature trying to find his way in the social environment seems to have nothing in common with the ideas of exploration, of meaning, of understanding, of rational consistency.
>
> (Tajfel, 1969, p. 79)

Thus, when we observe intergroup hostility (or even inter-group cooperation) we really need to appreciate how the group members understand the situation if we are to understand the intergroup perceptions. Tajfel proposed three important cognitive processes that were involved in prejudice. The first was *categorization*:

> There is no doubt that the contents of various stereotypes have their origins in cultural traditions, which may or may not be related to overgeneralized common experience, past or present. But what is more important is their general structure and function. As the late Gordon Allport (1954) and many others have pointed out, stereotypes arise from a process of categorization. They introduce simplicity and order where there is complexity and nearly random variation. They can help us to cope only if fuzzy differences between groups are transmitted into clear ones, or new differences created where none exist.
>
> (Tajfel, 1969, p. 82)

What Tajfel was saying here was that we take a dimension such as height, where there is a natural human variation, and that in perceiving people as 'tall' or 'short' we are reducing this variation to a limited set. We can then classify individuals as members of one of the groups, 'tall' and 'short'. (Notice the similarity of this process with the constructs of Kelly (1955) mentioned in Chapter 2.) Tajfel suggests that certain dimensions such as 'intelligent', 'lazy' or 'honest' are dimensions on which we group people. However, in making these classifications we tend to exaggerate the differences between groups and underrate the differences within groups. For example, people differ in varying degrees on friendliness, but in classifying one group as 'friendly' and another as 'unfriendly' we are likely to view the people in the 'friendly group' as much more friendly than people in the 'unfriendly group' (exaggerating any genuine differences between the groups), and we view the people in each group as more similar to each other on friendliness than they are (so reducing any genuine differences within a group).

The second cognitive process is *assimilation*:

> The content of the categories to which people are assigned by virtue of their social identity is generated over a long period of time within a culture ... The task of the social psychologist is to discover how these images are transmitted to individual members of society.
>
> (Tajfel, 1969, p. 86)

Tajfel argued that there are certain aspects of interperson perception that children acquire before others. We learn early on the groups of which we are a member and become aware of the relative position of our own group in society. So, the race and gender to which we belong are readily acquired and the value placed on them within the society we inhabit is readily communicated to us. (We shall return to the question of the cultural transmission of stereotypes in Chapter 7.)

The third cognitive process is the search for *coherence*:

> If an individual is to adjust to the flux of social change, he must attempt to understand it.
>
> (Tajfel, 1969, p. 92)

A girl wonders why her grandparents treat her differently to her brother. A man considers why he cannot get a job. A woman speculates on why so many changes have taken place in her country since she was a girl. Each of these people attempts to find explanations for their social circumstances. How they explain them is a question of *attribution*, which we considered in the last chapter. Tajfel suggests that the relative position between social groups requires explanation. We are unlikely to see these differences as accidental and hence attribute them to characteristics of the groups. Further, rather than looking at complex relationships we might simply explain social change and social position in terms of attributed inherent characteristics of the group members (such as *we are rich and powerful because we are clever and hard-working*). Finally, rather than seeing ourselves as responsible for a particular social position we may attribute the responsibility to the group (such as *I am out of work because it's a bad time for all car workers*), or to an outgroup (such as *I would not be out of work if THEY hadn't taken all our jobs*). Tajfel notes that in societies such as Victorian England or apartheid South Africa those of high status viewed themselves as inherently superior and other groups as inherently inferior as a way of justifying the advantages of their social position.

To examine whether prejudice emerges as a result of a *cognitive process* of group categorization we need to see what happens when groups are arbitrarily chosen, without competition or hostility existing between them (Tajfel, 1978b). Tajfel suggested that when we act in a prejudiced way we treat all members of an outgroup as the same and emphasize the difference between them and us. This appears to be what is happening when we categorize: we accentuate differences between groups (and underestimate differences within groups).

One aspect of categorization is that intergroup differences may be accentuated. Tajfel and Wilkes (1963) showed this quite clearly in a very simple experiment. Participants were asked to judge the lengths of eight lines of differing lengths. For some of the participants a large letter A appeared above the four longest lines, and B above the four shortest lines. When they were asked to judge the differences between the lines they overestimated the difference between the shortest A line and the longest B line compared to other participants who did not have the labels or had the labels randomly allocated to the lines. Simply labelling the long lines as A and the short lines as B had led to an accentuation of the difference at the boundary of the categories. Tajfel (1969) argued that this overestimation of intergroup differences arises in social perception as well: differences between the groups will be accentuated.

Support for this view came from Taylor *et al.* (1978). Participants listened to a group discussion, observing slides of the discussants. They were later asked to rate the group members on various characteristics and also recall who said what in the discussion. The discussion groups were made up of men and women or black men and white men. The results showed that gender and race were used to encode information about the discussants and that, in recalling who said what, more intragroup errors were made than intergroup errors: that is, with three men and three women in a discussion, the participants might make an error and attribute a statement from the discussion to the wrong person but, importantly, if it was said by a woman (for example) they were much more likely to attribute it to another woman rather than to one of the men.

Evidence of the accentuation of both intergroup differences and intragroup similarity was found by McGarty and Penny (1988) in their study. Participants were asked to rate political statements on a 100-point scale going from left-wing to right-wing. In one condition – uninformative label – half the statements were labelled author A and half labelled author B. In another condition – informative label – author A was described as right-wing and author B as Marxist. In a third condition – no label – there was no label with the statements. Accentuation of intergroup differences was found for both label conditions when the statement ratings were compared to the ratings in the no label condition. In the informative label condition the range of ratings within a group was smaller than both the uninformative label and no label condition. So when the labels were right-wing and Marxist the ratings within a group were more similar than for the other conditions, indicating ratings of intragroup similarity.

Ingroup favouritism

While Tajfel (1969) argued for the consideration of the cognitive factors in prejudice, the question arises of whether we get ingroup favouritism without proposing a Freudian personality dynamic or direct intergroup competition. In the *minimal group paradigm* (Tajfel, 1970; Tajfel *et al.*, 1971; Billig and Tajfel, 1973) people are assigned to one of two groups on an unimportant criterion, such as their preference for slides they were shown of paintings by Klee or Kandinsky, to provide a 'Klee group' and a 'Kandinsky group'. (In reality the assignment of participants to the two groups was random.) Each participant was then asked to assign 'money'

to two other participants identified only on their group membership. A clear finding was that the participants consistently
favoured their own group members. Interestingly, the choices were
set up so that the participants could give a relatively high amount
of money to both an ingroup member and an outgroup member,
or could give them both less but the ingroup member received
relatively more than the outgroup member. Rather than maxi-
mizing the *amount* they gave to both ingroup and outgroup
members the participants chose to maximize the *difference* in
favour of the ingroup.

Social identity theory

Why does such strong ingroup favouritism arise even in such
minimal group cases? The key to this is that *we* are a member of
the ingroup: it is a characteristic of our social self. It is the groups
to which we belong that establish our *social identity*: who we are
in our society, such as woman, Asian, grandmother, accountant,
golf club member, gay, Ford driver, etc. Further, group membership is associated with self-esteem, in that if we belong to a
favoured group then it will reflect positively on our social identity.
Thus, it is in our (self) interest to perceive our own group (the
ingroup) as more favourable to, and distinct from, other groups
(the outgroups) as this will give us a positive social identity.
However, people in other groups will have this same tendency as
well (viewing their own group favourably at the expense of other
groups, including our own). As a result prejudice (the derogation
of other groups) arises from the *social competition* of viewing one's
own group as better than others (Turner, 1975) even though there
may be no 'objective' competition for resources between the
groups. As Turner (1975) points out, ingroup favouritism (and
outgroup discrimination) arises in the minimal group paradigm not
from the particular groups selected by the experimenters but
because in the limited context of the study it was the only categorization that the participants could use to enhance their social
identity through ingroup favouritism.

These, and other studies, are the basis of the *social identity theory* of Tajfel and Turner (1979). Tajfel and Turner did not reject the concept of *personal identity* through which we can view ourselves as unique individuals with idiosyncratic attitudes and actions, rather they focused on the relationship between group membership and identity: *social identity*. Whilst not all social relations are based on our group membership, clearly many are: we are viewed by others and view ourselves in terms of gender, ethnicity, occupation and so on. We are conscious of ourselves as group members and by viewing the groups we belong to positively (in contrasting them with other groups) we are able to enhance our social identity. And so the (cognitive) process of social categorization in combination with the (motivational) desire for a positive social identity leads to ingroup favouritism and outgroup discrimination. One implication of this is that, if we are unable to achieve a positive social identity through membership of the groups we currently belong to, then we may attempt to become members of groups where we can achieve a more positive social identity.

Stereotyping and social identity theory

We can see that the cognitive process of categorization emphasizes the difference between groups, so ingroup members can view outgroup members as more different than they really are: *they are not like us*. Furthermore, with differences within groups underestimated, ingroup members can see the outgroup members as more similar than they really are: *they are all the same*. This will result in the individuals in a group being viewed in terms of their group membership. Finally, with the motivational process of a positive ingroup bias then the outgroup will be seen in (relatively) negative terms: *we are better than them*. Essentially, social identity theory argues that, through the cognitive processes of categorization and grouping, the ingroup members will develop a stereotypical view of the outgroup members (viewing them in terms of their outgroup identity), and through the motivational process of seeking to maintain a relatively high social identity the stereotype of outgroup members will tend to be negative.

The complexity of ingroup favouritism and outgroup discrimination

Not all groups are the same

Outside the psychology laboratory social groups have a number of differences that can influence the conditions for ingroup favouritism and outgroup discrimination. Some groups are of higher *status* than others within a society, so both groups may agree that company directors are of higher status than company cleaners. Status differentials may remain *stable* between groups or vary over time. As an example, professional soccer players have risen in status over the last decade in Britain. Some groups have clear boundaries, such as nationality, where it is clear who is a member and who is not; others do not, such as 'young people' (a footballer is old at 35, and a prime minister is young at 45). Some groups are easier to become a member of than others. It is easier to become a teacher than an airline pilot, and a short-sighted person is barred from the latter but not the former. The position of some groups in society may be seen as *legitimate* in that their status is accepted by other groups, such as the status of doctors. All these and other factors will influence how a person views the groups of which they are members (Tajfel, 1978c). But, generally speaking, people within high-status groups have a stronger ingroup favouritism than lower-status group members (Mullen *et al.*, 1992).

We must be careful in considering the conditions for ingroup favouritism, as it has been shown that it is not a global effect on all dimensions of comparison (e.g. van Knippenberg, 1984; Mummendey and Schreiber, 1983, 1984). Group members do not always rate themselves highest on every dimension. Outside the psychology laboratory, groups are more complex and the effects of categorization may be different. Clearly there are occasions when there is an agreement on the characteristics of groups on the basis of commonly accepted knowledge. For example, both doctors and nurses are likely to rate doctors as wealthier and having more surgical skill than nurses, simply on what both groups know about the different salary levels and training of the two occupations. Thus, a low-status group may be less antagonistic to a higher-status group it sees as *legitimate*, such as nurses' perceptions of doctors, but more antagonistic if it views the position of the higher-status group as *illegitimate*, such as an oppressed ethnic group in a racist society.

The ingroup is viewed as better on the 'important' dimensions

There are consensual dimensions on which group members from both groups agree as to which group is better, and competitive dimensions on which group members claim their own group is better (van Knippenberg, 1984). For example, both arts and science students might agree that science students are more numerate than arts students. Furthermore groups might acknowledge existing *status* differences, so students at a lower-status university have been shown to agree that students at a higher-status university are more self-assured and higher achievers than themselves (Spears and Manstead, 1989). However, the groups might also acknowledge other dimensions on which the low-status group is superior. Both groups rated the students at the lower-status university as more practically-minded and politically aware. Interestingly, in this study the two student groups were very much in agreement as to which group was better on which characteristic, indicating shared stereotypes of the two groups. However, the group members can still regard their group as superior if they identify with the characteristics on which their group is rated more highly. The students at the lower-status university might argue: *they may be full of themselves and know how to get what they want BUT we are practical, down-to-earth and know what's going on in the world.* Mummendey and Schreiber (1983, 1984) refer to this as the *different but better* strategy. In this way group members acknowledge the outgroup as superior on certain dimensions but maintain their own superiority on the ones that are important to their own social identity. Thus, arts students, in accepting that science students are more numerate than themselves, may not value numeracy as much as other characteristics such as creativity and spontaneity on which they are rated higher. In accepting a stereotype of themselves, and valuing certain dimensions as more important than others, group members can maintain a positive identity.

Personal identification with the group

Tajfel (1978c) argued that a person is committed to a group that enhances social identity. When this does not occur the person may seek to leave the group. Unhappy as an accountant a person might retrain to be a teacher (or vice versa). There will be situations when leaving the group may be difficult or impossible (it is not easy to change nationality, for example) so the person might seek to find features of the group that can be viewed positively. Essentially we identify with those social groups through which we gain a positive social identity, so a person working in a café while 'between jobs' as an actor may identify more with the actor/actress group than the waiter/waitress group.

According to social identity theory people with a strong personal identification with a group should also show high ingroup favouritism. Unfortunately for the theory, Hinkle and Brown (1990) did not find a strong relationship between strength of group identification and ingroup favouritism. They showed (Brown *et al.*, 1992) that the relationship is greatest for *collectivist* and *relational* groups. A collectivist group is one where working cooperatively for the success of the group is important, such as in a traditional Japanese company, as opposed to an individualist group where success can be achieved more readily through individual activity, such as in a used-car sales team where each sale yields a personal commission. (We will pick up on the collectivist–individualist dimension in Chapter 7.) A relational (as opposed to autonomous) group is one where the relative position of one's group compared to other groups is important, such as with the fans of a league football team. The significant findings of the study indicated that exhibiting strong ingroup favouritism was essentially a feature of collectivist groups rather than being general to all groups.

Crossed categories

We are all members of more than one category and sometimes there are categories that cross over each other. If there are four people in a room – a female doctor, a male doctor, a female nurse and a male nurse – then the categories of doctor/nurse cut across the categories male/female. Deschamps and Doise (1978) studied a group of boys and girls seated around a table working on a number of tasks. They found the expected outgroup discrimination when the children rated their performance on the tasks. The boys rated the boys higher than the girls and the girls rated the girls higher than the boys. However, when half the boys and half the girls were given red pens and the others blue pens, to produce a red group and a blue group crossed with boys/girls, the outgroup discrimination disappeared. This study has implications for reducing prejudice as it implies that ingroup favouritism can be reduced by the cross categories. We shall see how the introduction of new groupings may be effective (the common ingroup identity model – see below). However, as Brown (1995) points out, outside the laboratory it has been shown that some categories, such as gender or religion, may dominate over a second categorization and a bias remains.

Defining oneself by one's group: self-categorization theory

A development of social identity theory which attempts to deal with these complex group perceptions is *self-categorization theory* (Turner, 1987), which focuses on the groups that we see ourselves as belonging to. Turner argues that the way we see ourselves (our 'self-concept') depends on the categories with which we define ourselves. Furthermore, we can understand group behaviour in terms of the personal and social identities in which individuals categorize themselves. The theory concerns the person's definition of themself, their own self-concept. Self-categorization theory draws on Rosch's ideas of category levels and prototypes (see Chapter 2). Categories can be at different levels of abstraction (such as robin, bird, animal, living creature). Similarly, I can categorize myself at different levels: as an individual with my own set of characteristics that distinguish me from other individual people (likes coffee, paints badly, talks a lot, etc.), or in terms of the groups of which I am a member (male, psychologist, lecturer, etc.), or even as a member of the human race. The theory can be seen as a development of social identity theory as it also considers an individual's membership of social groups on self-categorization.

Turner accepts, like Tajfel, that categorization leads to the accentuation of intergroup differences and intragroup similarity. However, if the salient categorization is based on social identity (say, 'doctors' as opposed to 'hospital managers', and the person is a doctor) then there will be a tendency for the person to perceive themselves in terms of the stereotype of the social group to which they belong. Turner refers to this as *depersonalization*. To this extent the person engages with the hospital administrators *as a doctor* rather than as a specific individual with their own personal wants and desires. We can see this as an instance of 'self-stereotyping'.

Categorization, salience and 'fit'

Which categories are salient at any particular time depends on both the person and the situation they find themselves in. The category of nationality might not be salient to a British person in Britain but the same person abroad might find the category very salient. Categories also have to be *accessible* in that they must be readily available for the person to employ (Oakes *et al.*, 1991). Turner suggests that our perception of similarity and difference will lead to the use of particular categories (Turner, 1991). If a person perceives a dimension which distinguishes between two groups of people, and furthermore the differences between the two groups are perceived as greater than the differences within the groups, then that is likely to be a salient category. In a hospital meeting a doctor might perceive the doctor–manager dimension as much more salient than old–young or male–female. The same doctor might choose different categorizations when going to her child's school (parents, teachers) compared to taking part in the hospital meeting (doctors, hospital managers).

Turner calls the relationship of perceived intergroup differences to perceived intragroup differences the *meta-contrast ratio*, and the larger it is the more salient the category (Turner, 1991). In a hospital meeting with doctors, nurses, managers and accountants a number of categorizations are possible at different levels: see Figure 1 below.

Dr Brown perceives the (average) difference between the clinicians and the administrators to be large, but the (average) difference within the groups to be small (the doctors and nurses are similar; the accountants and managers are similar), producing a large meta-contrast ratio. So the clinician/administrator grouping will be salient in the meeting.

Even though the meta-contrast ratio can predict the level of categorization that will be salient, a second element is important in determining whether a particular categorization fits the situation: *normative fit* (Oakes *et al.*, 1991). To what extent do the actions of the people in the meeting fit the administrator/clinician

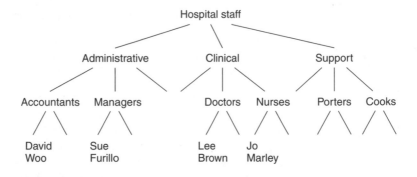

Figure 1 Levels of categories in the hospital example

categories in terms of the *social meanings* of the actions of the people involved? What we expect administrators and clinicians to say and do depends on what is viewed as *prototypical* of that group in this particular context (Oakes *et al.*, 1997). Let us assume the managers and accountants to be prototypically concerned with running an efficient hospital, and the doctors and nurses to be prototypically concerned with patient care. If the administrators are arguing for financial restraint to stop the hospital running over budget and the clinicians are arguing for more money for patient care, then the categorization provides a high level of normative fit.

When there is a salient categorization and a high level of normative fit then the expressed attitudes and behaviours of the group members are viewed in a stereotypical way (Oakes *et al.*, 1991). The clinicians may view the administrators, concerns about the hospital budget as: *typical administrators always concerned with money rather than caring about patients!* And the administrators might view the clinicians as: *they happily spend all this money on expensive treatments without thinking about where it all comes from.* Stereotypes in this view can be seen as the cognitive representations of social groups (Oakes *et al.*, 1991, p. 142). But notice that in other contexts these social groups will not 'fit' the situation so well. Dr Brown and hospital manager Furillo might view each other very differently when they are in a meeting together facing the members of the hospital Governing Board to discuss the financial situation.

Stereotyping

In the previous chapters we have focused on stereotyping as a cognitive bias. In Tajfel's work we can interpret the accentuation of ingroup similarity and outgroup discrimination as a cognitive bias as well. However, these accentuation effects are interpreted differently in self-categorization theory. Stereotypes reflect the perceived 'realities' (Haslam and Turner, 1992) of the groups in terms of the specific *context* of the person's judgement. The stereotypical views within the meeting of the clinicians and the administrators (above) reflect the reality of the categorization made by the people at the time. This is because the categorization made by the perceiver is a 'fit' to the context and behaviours of the people in the situation (Oakes and Reynolds, 1997).

Context is important as it influences the categorization of another person as an ingroup member or an outgroup member. An important factor in the context is the *frame of reference* (Haslam and Turner, 1992). This is the range of alternative positions available on the salient dimension and will have an impact on the meta-contrast ratio. Consider Dr Brown viewing manager Furillo. In the meeting with the nurses and administrators let us assume that the frame of reference is narrow (see Figure 2) and Furillo is seen by Dr Brown as an outgroup member (a stereotypical uncaring administrator). But when the frame of reference is extended, in the Governing Board meeting, now Furillo may be seen by Dr Brown as an ingroup member (fighting to maintain the level of patient care).

Self-categorization theory does not exclude individuals being viewed as individuals as opposed to group members. So when Brown and Furillo have a drink in a bar and talk about the local football team or their holiday plans, Brown may well view Furillo

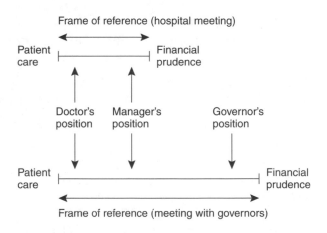

Figure 2   Context and stereotyping

as an individual. In self-perception terms the context and the behaviour do not lead Brown to categorize Furillo as a fellow hospital team member or an administrator but as an individual. This situation, like all others, leads to the particular level of categorization (Oakes and Reynolds, 1997). So we can see from this that, within self-categorization theory, stereotyping is a flexible process. Perceiving people stereotypically in terms of a particular group membership will depend very much on contextual factors: not only the categories employed but also the normative fit of the actions taking place to those categories.

Reducing bias between groups: the common ingroup identity model

Notice in the above example that the clinicians and administrators perceived each other as outgroup members in the hospital meeting but as ingroup members when in the Governors' meeting. This recategorization of outgroup members as members of a different ingroup as a way of reducing bias between groups is central to the *common ingroup identity model* (Gaertner *et al.*, 1993). In this model cooperation between members of separate groups can lead to a reduction in the bias between groups as it facilitates the members of the two groups perceiving themselves more as members of a single group and viewing the previously outgroup members more favourably. In an unpublished study, cited in Anastasio *et al.* (1997), students from the University of Delaware were asked to rate a videotape of a stereotypical outgroup member (a local young man who did not go to the university – referred to as a 'Townie') whom they were expecting to meet with other Townies after the study. In one condition the experimenters emphasized the 'student'/Townie grouping, but in a second condition they added the additional group of 'Delawareans', making it clear that the students and townspeople in the study were all part of this superordinate group. After watching the video the students rated the Townie viewed on video and Townies in general on a number of characteristics. As predicted by the researchers, the students in the two conditions rated the Townie on the video similarly, but those in the Delawarean condition not only saw themselves more as Delawareans than the students in the first condition but also rated Townies in general less stereotypically.

As Dovidio *et al.* (1997a) argue, contact between groups is most likely to reduce prejudice in a situation where the two groups can develop a common superordinate category. We can see that this develops our understanding of the *contact hypothesis* (Chapter 4). Evidence that the contact needs to be made between groups of equal status, that the interaction needs to be cooperative, and that members of one group can get to know the members of the other group can be interpreted in terms of encouraging the establishment of a new categorization of the members of the two groups as members of a single group.

Complexity in self-perception: within-group differentiation

Deschamps and Devos (1998), drawing on a number of studies by Deschamps over many years, argue that there are examples where the more one identifies with a group does not necessarily lead to seeing oneself as more like the others in the group (as self-categorization theory predicts through depersonalization). As we have seen above, when making a categorization between one's own group and an outgroup an individual will show ingroup favouritism. But according to Deschamps and Devos (1998) intragroup similarity – seeing the ingroup members as more similar than they are – may not occur. They argue that ingroup favouritism covaries with *autofavouritism*: that is, the person views their own group favourably over an outgroup but sees themselves as a better group member than other members of the ingroup. For example, an arts student might see arts students as better than science students but also see themselves as better than other art students. Thus, it is proposed that there are occasions where it is less relevant for a person to see themselves as different from an outgroup (*of course we arts students are different to science students*) than as different from other group members (*but I am particularly creative and spontaneous in my artistic work*).

Summary

Stereotyping is an intergroup process. Tajfel established that the categorization process can lead to the accentuation of between-group differences and within-group similarity. Combined with ingroup favouritism in establishing our social identity, outgroups tend to be perceived in a stereotypical manner. However, ingroup favouritism does not always occur due to the complex nature of groups. Self-categorization theory argues that, by focusing on the social group we perceive ourselves to be a member of at any particular moment, stereotypes reflect the realities of the groups at that particular moment. However, we will categorize ourselves as a member of different groups at different times dependent on a number of factors, such as the category accessibility, meta-contrast ratio and fit. Viewing outgroup members as part of a common ingroup may lead to a reduction in the discrimination towards them. Finally, self-categorization theory may, like social identity theory, underestimate the complexity of the social identity process.

Further reading

Abrams, D. and Hogg, M.A. (eds) (1999) *Social identity and social cognition*. Oxford: Blackwell. This book provides an account of links between social cognition research and that in the field of social identity.

Worchel, S., Morales, J.F., Páez, D. and Deschamps, J.-C. (eds) (1998) *Social identity – international perspectives*. London: Sage. This is a detailed review of social identity research by authors from Europe, North America and Australia.

The language
of stereotyping

Introduction

IN THE BOOK SO FAR I have emphasized cognition in explanations of stereotypes. Essentially they are viewed as internal
mental structures (schemas, prototypes) that develop through the
way human beings process information (categorization, limited
capacity). Thus, the person, through the working of their cognitive processes, acquires stereotypes in their understanding of
individuals belonging to social groups. In this chapter I will be
considering an alternative approach to the cognitive explanation
of stereotypes within psychology.

Let us consider an example. Two colleagues are talking
about a third:

'Alberto said he had a good time at the opera last night.'
'Ah, the Italians do love music.'
'You are so right.'

We can argue that this little snippet of conversation can be
explained within a cognitive explanation by viewing both speakers
as knowing the stereotype of Italians as classical-music-lovers. The
stereotype leads to their explanation of why Alberto had a good
time at the opera: *because Italians like classical music and he is
Italian*. The explanation arises effortlessly, quickly and without
requiring much thought. However, the attribution might be
biased: Alberto may hate opera music but had a great time with
a new girlfriend, or was given free seats in a box and enjoyed
the event despite not normally liking opera. Given more time and
motivation a more 'accurate' explanation might be developed by
considering whether Alberto likes other operas or whether other
people like this one and so forth. Thus, the explanation framework of the cognitivist theorist is based on the cognitive structures
and processes that it is inferred led to the statements being made.

An alternative way of viewing the conversation is to focus on explanations in terms of language. As Cauthern *et al.* (1971) pointed out stereotypes are essentially linguistic behaviours that vary with social class and nationality. It is within language that stereotypical ideas are expressed: conversations, newspaper articles, discussions, and so on. But note that, in the above example, the words spoken are viewed as a direct manifestation of the schema of Italians. It is not the words that are of interest but the mental state they appear to confirm. An alternative view argues that this is a naive view of language. 'Discourse [is] a *social practice* in itself, as opposed to a neutral transmitter, with its own characteristic features and practical consequences' (Wetherell and Potter, 1988, p.168). We can take this further and argue that we do not need to infer universal mental structures in our psychological explanation; rather we can attempt to understand the function of the discourse (Wetherell and Potter, 1988). Why was the conversation constructed in this way by these two people? The speakers may have been using irony – or they may have been reporting Alberto's ironic use of the term 'good time'. It may be difficult to decide on the functions of a particular discourse and therefore a certain amount of interpretation is necessary. If I make the statement 'pass the sauce' at a meal it may appear an innocuous request, but if you have just made a delicate French meal it might be the greatest insult I can offer. Even my 'umm, lovely' can have a rich range of meanings. Am I expressing my genuine pleasure in the meal? Am I simply following a social rule of politeness? Am I being sarcastic? Consider the variety of meanings in a statement such as: 'it's not like mother used to make'.

Antaki (1988) distinguishes these two approaches by the different explanations of social events sought. In one case, the researchers are attempting to find out the *private* internal mental framework of the person which causes them to perceive a social event in a particular way, such as in the social cognition theories of stereotyping. Here the way perceivers process information is examined through controlled studies such as presenting a brief vignette about a person and noting the inferences the perceiver makes about that person. An aspect of the vignette is changed and the effect of that change on the perceiver's judgement is observed. If the perceiver, acting as a mock juror, rates a person as more likely to be guilty when they are described as being a member of a particular ethnic group, then researchers argue that the information processing is 'biased' by the stereotype of that group. In the second case, the researchers are endeavouring to understand explanations for social events communicated *publicly*. Here conversations, speeches, texts, all present accounts of the social world. We can look at what someone says to their friends in a café about a social group or look at the speeches made by a politician. We can analyse these accounts to see how they represent people and events. Why has the person chosen to say this in this way? Politicians, newspapers and defendants in court cases are obvious examples of where a person may put a particular 'spin' on what they are saying to serve a particular function. The politician wants to convince the public of the 'sense' of their views: the government politician wants to present him- or herself as being in control of the economy, whereas the opposition politician wants to present the government as incompetent in running the economy. In this approach it is the language used (the text) that is the data, and the researcher seeks to uncover its function (intention of the speaker or writer) through an examination of the arguments employed in the discourse. It is the second of these two forms of explanation that will be the focus of this chapter.

The 'turn to the text'

An important point to note here is that the 'turn to the text' (Burman and Parker, 1993, p. 7) is not simply seen by its proponents as an interesting alternative methodology but as a completely radical reformulation of psychology itself. According to this view, it is within discourse that concepts used in psychology are constructed (such as 'personality', 'identity', 'attentional mechanisms' and even our 'selves'). These:

> are not things hiding inside the person which the psychologist can then 'discover' but are created by the language

used to describe them. Psychological phenomena have a public and collective reality, and we are mistaken if we think that they have their origin in the private space of the individual.

(Burman and Parker, 1993, p. 1)

This approach attacks the basic tenets of traditional psychology which seeks to find internal psychological causes for behavioural effects.

The inevitability of stereotyping due to the nature of cognition?

Particularization

In the middle of the twentieth century stereotyping was seen as something done by unintelligent people who were to be discouraged by campaigns to educate people to stop it (Brown, 1965). However, much of the cognitive work considered up to now holds that categorization is a key to perception and that stereotyping follows from our categorical perception of other people, either because the processes of cognition require us to process information efficiently and/or to avoid overloading our cognitive systems, or because the way we perceive social categories helps to maintain a positive social identity. Thus, stereotyping is a characteristic of us all. Billig (1985, 1987) notes the implication that, in this model of stereotyping, prejudice is inevitable. If stereotyping is fundamental to the way we think then we cannot avoid being prejudiced.

Billig (1985) questioned some of the key assumptions of this approach, such as whether prejudice follows inevitably from the nature of perception. If we need to simplify the information available to us in order to perceive it, and the resultant categorization leads to prejudice, why is it that we are prejudiced against groups of people we have never experienced? For example, in one study participants had no difficulty assigning characteristics to thirty-five nationalities despite the fact that three of the nationalities were bogus and made up for the study (Hartley, 1946). In general these three groups were assigned negative characteristics. Billig (1985) suggests that prejudice could lead to categorization rather than the other way round. With a prejudiced view of foreigners, people may then categorize an unknown nationality in a negative way. Billig (1985) makes a second point about perception: whilst all animals perceive, it makes sense to view prejudice as unique to human beings. We also express our prejudice through language, also specific to human beings. Thus prejudice may not be a fundamental feature of perception. Rather we are able to use language flexibly. We can use it to simplify the world and to communicate our prejudices. But we can also convey tolerance through language and develop complexity.

Billig (1985) suggests that the human thinker has been seen in a rather restricted way, doomed to interpret experience in stereotypical terms due to the basic cognitive processes in operation. He argues that we are more flexible than this, able to categorize information in more than one way. Faced with a 40-year-old woman doctor driving a sports car, how do I categorize her? As a woman? As a doctor? As a sports car owner? What leads to the choice of a particular category? This is crucial to Billig's argument: along with categorization we must have *particularization*, where we make a selection of particular categories or particular subcategories or particular examples. For example, a person may make the distinction between 'career women' and 'housewives' when arguing about the nature of the category 'women', or choose particular examples such as Hillary Clinton or their own mother. It is not that prejudiced people are more simplistic in their thinking than tolerant people, argues Billig, but that they choose particular categorizations to support their prejudiced view. In Billig's (1987) *rhetorical approach to thinking* it is not that prejudiced and tolerant people differ in the complexity of their thought but that they differ in the arguments they construct to support their beliefs. If we look at the language people use in their arguments we can observe the *rhetoric* (the persuasive points) employed to support their views. A sexist might claim that a successful woman was successful due to her 'womanly wiles' rather than on merit, in an attempt to undermine her achievement and maintain a prejudiced view of women's competence. Similarly, as Flew (1975) points out, a chauvinist Scotsman might argue that 'no Scotsman would do that' on finding out that an Englishman had committed a specific crime. When faced with the counter-evidence – that a Scotsman had committed such a crime – the chauvinist might use the argument: 'he is not a *true* Scotsman'! Billig (1985) noted that prejudiced participants in Adorno *et al.*'s (1950) study on the authoritarian personality also made this type of distinction, with anti-Semitic participants arguing for a difference between 'good' and 'bad' Jews.

Prejudice is not inevitable if we regard human thought as more flexible than implied by the view that categorization is required for perception and prejudice is an outcome of categorization. Furthermore, a categorization can always be opposed by a particularization. People are inventive in supporting their views (Billig, 1985) and when we analyse the text of what someone says or writes we can examine the rhetorical arguments they are using to support their views. In this approach prejudice is not an outcome of the 'natural process of cognition' but is the result of the different views held by prejudiced and tolerant people.

Categorization

Potter and Wetherell (1987) question three assumptions that are made within the cognitive view that categorization arises from perception, that is, that it is a 'natural' process in making sense of the world. First, they question the assumption that categories are 'preformed' and enduring – that is, we have a set of prototypes for different categories and we slot people into appropriate categories. Second, they question the assumption that categories have fixed structures organized around prototypes. Third, they question the assumption that categorization simplifies and hence biases our perceptions of people in a stereotypical way.

Potter and Wetherell (1987) examined accounts of people describing others and looked at the way that categorizations were employed. They argued that there was a lot of variability in the

way categories were used in these accounts and that often categories were chosen by the person to justify or assign blame in
their explanation of events. They drew on their own research into
the category Maori in accounts by middle-class, European New
Zealanders to show the high degree of variability in the characteristics associated with the category across different respondents
and different topics. The range of descriptions and the subtle
differences between them would be lost by attempting to 'shoe-
horn' the descriptions into some form of generalization of the
category. Furthermore there were clear inconsistencies between
accounts, with Maoris described as both lazy and hard-working
and proud and humble.

In a second example, examining the concept of 'community'
in accounts of a 1980 'riot' in the city of Bristol where fighting
took place between the police and local youth, Potter and
Wetherell showed that, whilst there was common agreement on
the characteristics of 'community', it was applied differently in
different explanations. In one set of explanations the police were
considered as part of the community and the proposed solution
was to bring them closer to other members of the community. In
another set of explanations the police were viewed as outside the
community and attacking it, with the solution being for them to
be less antagonistic to it (i.e. less repressive and less racist).

Potter and Wetherell also drew upon the work of Billig on
particularization (described above) to argue against the view that
prejudice is a 'natural' outcome of categorization. In conclusion
they propose that categorization does not determine how we view
an event but that we draw on categories to assign blame, justify
and legitimize the accounts we construct to explain people and
events. Consider a conversation where a person tells a friend that
John hit Brian in a bar last night. The reply 'John is a thug'
constructs the event as the action of a bully. John is not a nice
person. But consider an alternative construction of the event: 'I'm
not surprised, Brian has had it coming for a long time.' Now here
John's action is constructed as that of a man at the end of his
tether or simply as what anyone else would do when faced with
someone like Brian. The way John and Brian are viewed and their

actions constructed by the two friends can be interpreted from their discourse: the words chosen and the meanings constructed in the language employed.

The construction of meaning

The cognitive approach to social perception has followed Lippmann's view that the individual's cognitive processes are not able to appreciate the full complexity of social experience and so we simplify it through categorization. Thus, we develop a restricted or distorted view of the social world: we stereotype. The focus of this view is on the individual and the mental processing taking place within them. Knowledge and under-standing of others arise from the information available to us and the limitations of our information processing system.

It has been argued that this view ignores the 'social' in social psychology: that is, that social knowledge does not arise as the end product of an individual's cognitive processes but that we create understanding through our social interactions. Knowledge is socially constructed (Gergen, 1985). How do I (an English person) view the Italians? Rather than examining my prototype of Italians we can look at how I construct them in discourse. What do I say about them in conversation? How do I describe different Italians in different conversations with different people? Most importantly, I do not make these utterances into a void: I am speaking in a context, to a particular audience, be it talking with my friends in a bar comparing Italian and Brazilian soccer teams, or talking at a political meeting about the Italian head of the European Union. The things I say gain their meaning through the social relationships I have with the other people. It is within these social relationships, such as friends or fellow English people, that the meanings will be negotiated.

The social constructionist view (see Burr, 1995) argues for the importance of language in the way in which meaning is nego-tiated. Not only is our use of language important (as we saw above in Billig's work on the way people argue for their views),

but also the way in which the language structures the meanings constructed. Contained within language are culturally-based subtleties of meaning.

The language of stereotyping

Consider the word 'boy'. My dictionary rather tersely describes it as 'a male child'. Yet there is more to the word than this simple definition. Spike the dog in a *Tom and Jerry* cartoon pats his pup on the head and proudly proclaims: that's my boy! Enshrined in our understanding of this is the father's pride in the son and heir. Yet consider the use of the term by a bigoted white policeman in a small town in the American South to a black detective in the 1960s (as portrayed in the 1967 film *In the Heat of the Night*). Here the meaning is entirely pejorative. The black detective is not being considered as a college-educated experienced detective who may help solve a murder case but as a childlike inferior. The term is used to maintain a racist power relationship and undermine the clear intellectual superiority of the black detective. Thus, language is not value-free, and through the use of language we construct certain social meanings.

As Harré (1988) points out, social relationships are encoded in language itself. In English the pronoun 'you' has become a general form of reference, but a number of languages have maintained a formal form of address ('Sie' in German, 'vous' in French) and a familiar form ('du' in German, 'tu' in French). How you address someone reflects status. Just as Ron Jones, the boss, will refer to John Smith, the doorman, as 'John' but expect to be called 'Mr Jones' in return, a higher-status person will use the familiar form of address with lower-status individuals but will expect the formal form in return. Breaking the conventional use can lead to a person feeling insulted. As Harré (1988) points out, English does not encode the subtleties of social relations in the way that some languages do, and English speakers may employ nonverbal cues to indicate the speaker–listener relationship. However, this should not allow us to forget that languages such as

Japanese have a rich encoding of social relations within the language itself.

It is not just pronouns that can be used to indicate status. If an office manager refers to the 'lads' in the workshop or the 'girls' on the shop-floor the status difference is clear. Notice how unconventional it sounds to refer to 'the lads in the boardroom' or 'the girls in the government', as they both use familiar terms to refer to high-status people. Feminists have shown that language contains sexist assumptions (Burr, 1998). Women are referred to in more familiar terms than men (e.g. the girls and the guys), implying a lower, more childlike status. Female terms have a negative connotation ('spinster' as opposed to 'bachelor'). General terms like 'mankind' rather than 'human beings' make women less visible. High-status people may be referred to as though they are only men: 'the politicians and their wives' rather than 'politicians and their spouses'. Consider the use of the term 'office manager' in the second sentence of this paragraph. Did you assume a particular gender when you read it? Thus, language is *gendered*, frequently positioning women at a lower status than men (Burr, 1998).

Discourse analysis

Whilst the term *discourse analysis* has been used in a number of ways, Potter and Wetherell (1987) provide a helpful definition: discourse refers 'to all forms of spoken interaction, formal and informal, and written texts of all kinds. So when we talk of "discourse analysis" we mean analysis of any of these forms of discourse' (p. 7). They suggest that there are three key points to the analysis of discourse.

First, what is the *function* of the discourse? There is not a single function to language, such as simply to impart information. A speaker uses language for a purpose. Before an examination two students talk:

'I've not done much revision.'
'Me neither.'

What are they trying to achieve here? It could be that the first person does not want to be seen as a swot. They may be setting up an excuse for possible failure; or aiming to enhance their future success if they pass (having claimed to have done little revision). The second person may be just being polite in agreeing with the first. Language serves a function but will serve different functions in different contexts. The first student fails the examination and says to the tutor: 'I revised really hard for that examination but the wrong questions came up.' Notice here that we could analyse these accounts by saying that the student revised or did not revise: one statement must be true and the other false and we need to find which most closely reflects 'reality'. But this is not how discourse analysts would view the accounts. They would look at the contexts of the utterance and try and uncover the function of the statements. With the tutor, the student might be trying to present themselves as hard-working but unfortunate.

Second, the student is using language to *construct* different social 'realities'. In the first context the language is selected to negotiate a particular meaning with a fellow student, in the latter with the tutor. Conventional associations are reflected in the language chosen: students conventionally don't like students who work very hard but tutors conventionally do. Thus the language employed draws on these to serve its purpose for the speaker in order to 'construct versions of the social world' (Potter and Wetherell, 1987, p. 33). Language is constructive as well as constructed. Consider also how different politicians from different political parties would describe and explain the current state of the economy. Even though they are describing the 'same' state of affairs they are constructing different accounts of it. But, of course, it is not the 'same' state of affairs as their different accounts are different versions of the social world. Thus, the question of whether one account is more accurate than any other is not appropriate, as all we have are the different versions rather than 'true' and 'false' versions.

The third point is the *variation* in accounts (Potter and Wetherell, 1987). Different people, different contexts, different occasions will all lead to variation. Traditionally, psychology has

viewed variation as indicating either internal psychological phenomena or a source of error. For example, one group of participants
see a man perform a task and a second group observe a woman
performing the same task. The participants are asked to rate or
describe the competence of the actor. Variation between the
groups is indicative of the effect of the actor's gender on the
participants, and variation within the groups is taken as 'error'
as it is assumed that the participants in a group, chosen randomly
and viewing the same event, should perform in the same way. If
the variation between the groups exceeds variation within the
groups by a certain extent then a 'significant' effect of gender on
the participants is claimed, indicating that a gender stereotype is
biasing the perception. But, to Potter and Wetherell, this is not
acknowledging the general nature of the variability in the study:
the variations in the accounts (regardless of whether between
participants in the same group or different groups) reflect the
constructive nature of each account.

Interpretative repertoires

The discourse analyst will seek to analyse the linguistic 'texts' –
the various accounts – to work out the function of the language
used. However, as Wetherell and Potter (1988) point out, the
analyst is *interpreting* the text rather than being able to simply
pluck out the function, so the interpretation of the text is a process
of developing *hypotheses* about its functions. For example, did
the person say this as a justification? Thus, the analyst looks
closely at the text, attempting to draw out from it its function
and consequences. An important point here is that discourse
analysts focus on variation, as the different constructions of
the social world can be inferred and the different purposes of the
language proposed. Why did the student say they had revised in
one context and say they did not in another? In many cases the
variation provides a complex set of information that is difficult
to interpret (Wetherell and Potter, 1988).

However, despite the variation in accounts the analyst may
be able to draw out common themes or ideas expressed across

accounts. These are termed *interpretative repertoires* (Wetherell and Potter, 1988). In their own work on middle-class European New Zealanders' accounts of Maoris, Wetherell and Potter drew out a number of interpretative repertoires, with one key repertoire which they termed 'cultural fostering' identified in the accounts of 90 per cent of the participants. This repertoire indicated support for the development of Maori culture but also implied that it was necessary as the Maoris had not 'retained' a strong enough sense of identity. As Wetherell and Potter point out, the arguments within the repertoire, whilst not advocating a white supremacist view and while supportive of Maori culture, still retain a position where it is the Maoris who have the 'problem' and must regain their cultural identity rather than any change being required of the European New Zealanders.

This repertoire should not be viewed as a 'schema' of Maoris held by the European New Zealanders, as a number of different repertoires were employed by the participants. Also, the context and combination of repertoires provide an overall interpretation of the accounts in a complex way. For the European New Zealanders, through the selection of a number of key repertoires, they are able to present themselves as favourable to multiculturalism, at the same time as arguing against complaints of racism and the protests of Maoris, to achieve the function of maintaining a particular ideological position (Wetherell and Potter, 1988).

Analysing discourse

Potter and Wetherell (1987) describe a procedure for undertaking discourse analysis. The practical process of analysing discourse differs from the traditional empirical studies in social psychology. For example, the research questions proposed are not hypotheses to test out whether a theory can be rejected or not, nor to determine accuracy or bias. Rather the research questions are posed to draw out how the discourse is constructed and the functions it serves. Consider how we might examine discourse concerning 'the government funding of students'. We might draw on accounts from interviews carried out by the researchers, but texts could be taken from a number of sources such as newspapers or television programmes. The accounts need to be transcribed so that the analysis can take place. Then the texts are coded using a coding system that relates to the research question. This also reduces the material to a coded form for analysis. For example, the statements *graduates get high-paid jobs so students should fund themselves* and *companies like to employ graduates so students can expect a good job when they graduate* might be classified under the same code, and *it's not fair that poor students must spend all their free time working whereas rich students can focus on their studies* would be coded differently. There are no hard-and-fast rules to the coding – but it is an interactive process with the text. If the initial coding (attempting to draw out all references to student funding) does not seem to be adequate for the text, the coding can be altered. Now the coded material is analysed by looking for patterns of variability and similarity in the accounts. These patterns can be used to infer repertoires and make hypotheses as to the function of the accounts. The next step is to consider the validity of this analysis. Does it provide an adequate explanation of the discourse? Does it present the discourse as the participants (rather than just the analyst) view it? Does it generate new questions and develop new research? Also the work must be written in report form in such a way that a reader can examine how the analysis was undertaken and has the opportunity to question each stage of the procedure. Finally, Potter and Wetherell argue, the practical application of the work needs to be considered.

Discourse analysis and stereotypes

Within discourse analysis the 'fixed' stereotype associated with a categorization does not exist. In some contexts, in some accounts, people will use social categories in certain ways. For example, a person might say *students spend most of their time sitting around chatting*, but on another occasion they might say *my niece spends so much time studying at college*. Whereas the first statement might lead us to infer that the person holds the 'idle student' stereotype the latter statement appears to contradict it. But in discourse analytic terms the contradiction is not indicative of whether the person has the stereotype or not but is evidence of the variation in accounts. If we look at the context of the accounts we may be able to infer their function from an analysis of the discourse of which these are small fragments. In the first instance the function might be to justify a particular view of young people as not as responsible as their forebears, whilst in the second instance it may be to do with presenting one's family in a positive way.

In an example of discourse analysis, Gill (1993) examined broadcasters' accounts of why there were few women disc jockeys on their radio stations. Interestingly, the explanations focused on the audience (who were claimed to prefer male disc jockeys) and the women themselves (with claims that they did not apply for the posts or did not possess the appropriate skills). As Gill points out, the broadcasters' explanations of the lack of women disc jockeys allowed them to maintain that they were non-sexist by accounting for the injustice in terms of the women and the audience rather than the radio station and its practice of employing male disc jockeys. Like the European New Zealanders' accounts of Maoris the accounts allowed the participants to present themselves as not prejudiced whilst maintaining an ideological position that contained inequality within it.

Whilst the European New Zealanders and the broadcasters may be said to be employing stereotypes in that their accounts contain statements that we can label as stereotypical (e.g. *women do not have the background to be broadcasters*: see Gill, 1993, p. 83), the key point to note is that the statement does not indicate an underlying stereotype as an element within the person's cognition (Edwards and Potter, 1992), but that the statement, within the discourse, serves a function at that time in that context. On other occasions a variety of other statements will be made which may or may not be labelled as stereotypical. Indeed, according to discourse analysts, psychological explanations themselves (in terms of cognitive structures and processes) can be viewed as an ideological perspective presented within language

(Edwards and Potter, 1992). Whilst providing an important critique to the 'rigidity' in the cognitive view of stereotyping, discourse analysts, more radically, tend to remove the psychology out of stereotyping by dismissing explanations in terms of mental structures in favour of language (Reicher *et al.*, 1997).

Positioning theory

Harré and Secord (1972), following from Goffman (1959), showed how we can interpret social behaviour by looking at the *roles* people inhabit and the 'rules' (or social conventions) they employ. This is referred to as a dramaturgical standpoint, as social interaction is viewed as like a play with the actors in the play taking on certain roles. Consider a mother talking to her teenage son about tidying his room. We can understand their interaction by the roles of mother and son in our society and the conventions of mother/son interaction. We do not expect the woman to act in the same way with all men and boys. When the woman goes out for a meal with a man we may understand the situation if we see them in the 'anniversary treat' script, with a man who is her husband, or 'lovers' meeting', with a man who is not. We have learnt from others (such as *role models*) how to act in certain roles, such as mother, father, doctor, nurse.

Davies and Harré (1990) argue that the dramaturgical position limits the choice individuals have in the way they 'play' a particular role. As an alternative they use the term *subject-position* rather than role to allow the person more choice in their position within a social interaction. Social interaction is examined through discourse. Individuals construct meaning through discourse and discourse constructs the individual. Within a discourse concerning, say, 'gender' there are a number of different subject positions. Phrases like *women are able to achieve success on their own merits* and *women are better in the carer role* may place a person within a different subject-position within a discourse. An individual comprises the subject-positions taken up within the discourses in which they engage. According to Davies and Harré (1990),

143

person categories are important as we learn to use them to position ourselves within discourse: for example, *I am more of an introvert than you* or *I am in the boys' team* or *I am an accountant.* Categories of people both include some people and exclude others. Thus, through discourse, who we are (our 'self') is constructed.

Positioning theory (Davies and Harré, 1990) proposes that people are located at various subject-positions within conversations. Within a discourse we take up subject-positions to produce a 'story line'. For example, in a conversation between a lecturer and a student about an essay topic the participants are positioned by the categories of lecturer/student and their own personal histories. The student saying *can you advise me on what material to include?* positions the lecturer as expert and themselves as pupil. If the lecturer says *look at the paper I wrote last year criticizing Smith's work*, the lecturer is taking up a subject-position as expert. The positioning places the two speakers in this conversation in a social relationship where they are positioned at different levels of competence. Other conversations will position the speakers in different power relations. What is said in conversation allows us to position ourselves and others. In a political discourse individuals take part in a story line about, say, taxation policy, taking up positions that we might categorize somewhat simplistically as 'conservative' or 'left-wing'. 'Positioning can thus be understood as the discursive construction of personal stories that make a person's actions intelligible and relatively determinate as social acts and within which the members of the conversation have specific locations' (van Langenhove and Harré, 1994, p. 363).

As well as positioning ourselves and others within a discourse, a conversation presents versions of social knowledge through rhetorical reconstruction (van Langenhove and Harré, 1994). If a person says: *These people are simply a bunch of lazy scroungers. Look at the way they live. They cannot be bothered even to look after their neighbourhood* – then that speaker is presenting a version of the social world. They are reconstructing the knowledge of the people referred to through the rhetoric of the words spoken. Another speaker might say: *Look at these people. The police are constantly harassing them. They are not allowed proper health care. They are not allowed to get decent jobs. They are discriminated against at all levels of society.* Here the speaker is presenting another version of social knowledge.

Stereotypes are used by a speaker to position others within a particular story line. In a conversation amongst a group of friends one might say: *That doctor gave me only a couple of minutes. He didn't seem to care about my aches and pains. He was probably in a rush to get to the golf course.* Here the other speakers are 'invited to conform' (Davies and Harré, 1990) to this particular stereotype of doctors and may then take up the position of continuing this story line by telling anecdotes of uncaring doctors. Other speakers may not take up these positions and say, for example: *I have always found my doctor caring and helpful.* Yet within certain discourses, such as boss and employees, the power relationship is such that the listeners may feel obliged to conform, and the employees might nod in agreement with an insulting comment by the boss about doctors yet feel annoyed by it.

Van Langenhove and Harré (1994) make an important distinction between cultural stereotypes and personal stereotypes, which they distinguish on the public–private and individual–collective dimensions (see Figure 3). They argue that a cultural stereotype is a position in public discourse. An individual might draw on a particular cultural stereotype for their own purposes. So a person in argument might employ the stereotype 'lads' to imply that a group of young men are lovable rogues, or the stereotype 'skinheads' to imply that the young men are thugs, in the knowledge that these are cultural stereotypes. But certain ways of acting or describing others become habitual and privatized. A person may habitually describe young men in a negative way, often using the skinhead stereotype. Similarly, a person might develop a personal habit of decrying older men with appalling taste in clothing as 'red tie man', combining features of the 'fashion victim' and 'mutton dressed as lamb' stereotypes (after a former boss who always wore a red tie and was described as particularly badly dressed). Thus, we develop personal stereotypes. In expressing these personal stereotypes within discourse some may be taken up and used as positions by others. The person writes a popular novel based on their experiences at work called *The Man with the Red Tie* and through its use in public discourse the representation 'red tie man' may become a new cultural stereotype (like the term 'yuppie' that appeared in the 1980s).

A key point to note is that personal stereotypes are not viewed here as mental structures, such as schemas. If a person employs the 'skinhead' stereotype it does not mean that they believe all crop-headed young men are thugs, rather that they may often use this term to position themselves in certain conversations with others. But there will be situations where they might wish to position themselves differently in a conversation (such as when talking about a favoured nephew who has just had a cropped haircut) and they will choose not to employ the stereotype 'skinhead'.

We saw above that there may be a number of alternative conceptions of the same category. As an example, we might characterize doctors as caring, intelligent individuals working long hours who sometimes perform amazing feats of medicine. Alternatively we might see them as being in control of the medical profession, and using their power to make lots of money and spend as much time as they can on the golf course. Cultural stereotypes, according to van Langenhove and Harré (1994), are

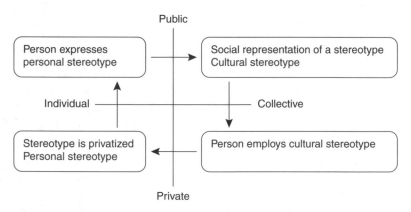

Figure 3   Cultural and personal stereotypes
(Source: van Langenhove and Harré, 1994, copyright Blackwell Publishers Ltd/Executive Management Committee of JTSB)

not distorted views of 'reality' but socially constructed representations of categories of people. It is not appropriate in this view to see one representation or another as right or wrong, as different representations are drawn on by speakers in the positioning of themselves (and others) in discourse. A doctor appealing for more public funding for a children's hospital may employ the 'hard-pressed, miracle-worker' doctor stereotype. A disgruntled patient having paid a large medical bill despite feeling no better might use the 'rich golfing' doctor stereotype in discussion with friends about the bill. The stereotype chosen from the repertoire of cultural representations of doctors will be the one that provides an appropriate character for the story line (van Langenhove and Harré, 1994) being developed by the speaker.

Interestingly, van Langenhove and Harré (1994) argue that individual category members that we meet, such as a new neighbour Mary who is a doctor, may not impact on our use of the social representations of doctor. Thus, stereotype change will not occur through encountering actual members of the category. Rather, change will occur with the formation of new social representations that then get used in discourse, or through changes in the positions taken within discourse. For example, consider changes in the way members of different ethnic groups have been characterized and positioned within children's stories (books, comics, films and television programmes) over the last hundred years. Alternatively, note how the term 'yuppie' is not often used now.

Conclusion

Whilst the traditional approach to psychology is unlikely to abandon its explanatory framework in terms of personal or internal explanations (such as personality, identity, or schema) as a result of the work on discourse, what the work has done, and is continuing to do, is to provide an important critique of some of the basic assumptions of the discipline that appear to 'justify injustice' (Gill, 1993) or imply that 'prejudice is natural' (Billig,

1985). It is true that cognitive theorists argue that the *contents* of stereotypes do change and that it is only the *process* that is relatively fixed (e.g. Fiske and Taylor, 1991), but it is important to remember that understanding variation in our accounts of people is as important as understanding consistency.

Summary

The examination of language has questioned some of the basic assumptions of the cognitive view of stereotyping. People may employ stereotypes to support their prejudices, not the other way around. Furthermore, people may employ variety in their descriptions of others, sometimes in apparent contradiction with each other, rather than a fixed stereotype. Language is not viewed as a medium for communicating knowledge but as the medium for constructing knowledge. An analysis of discourse can reveal its function and the ideological positions that exist within it. Positioning theory examines the way subject-positions are adopted within discourse. In this theory stereotypes are positioning devices within story lines rather than mental structures.

Further reading

The following books provide a more detailed account of the range of ideas introduced in this chapter:

Billig, M. (1987) *Arguing and thinking: a rhetorical approach to social psychology*. Cambridge: Cambridge University Press.
Burr, V. (1995) *An introduction to social constructionism*. London: Routledge.
Edwards, D. (1996) *Discourse and cognition*. London: Sage.
Harré, R. and van Langenhove, L. (eds) (1999) *Positioning theory*. Oxford: Blackwell.

Stereotypes and culture

Introduction

I N THE MID-1950S the Greek Cypriots campaigned for Enosis (union with Greece) against the British rulers of their island. The author Lawrence Durrell had lived in Greece for many years, developed a knowledge of the language and a love of the people. He had moved to Cyprus in 1953. Now he found himself Director of Information Services for the government. Four years later he published an account of his experience of the unfolding of the crisis. When the British hung a young Greek for the shooting of a policeman Durrell wrote:

> the image – the mythopoeic image of the Englishman which every Greek carried in his heart, and which was composed of so many fused and overlapping pictures – the poet, the lord, the quixotic and fearless defender of right, the just and freedom-loving Englishman – the image was at last thrown down and dashed into a thousand pieces, never again to be reassembled.
>
> (Durrell, 1957, p. 241)

Notice that Durrell was suggesting that the Greeks shared an image of 'the Englishman'. It was a shared or collective representation of the English known to all Greeks. But this image was not a representation of Durrell or any other specific, individual Englishman but a *mythopoeic* image – a constructed myth of the Englishman within Greek culture. The death of the young Greek had shattered that image.

My choice of this example is to illustrate the importance of culture to the stereotypes that we hold. We might wish to ask how the Greeks developed this image of the English, and look at the history of Anglo-Greek relations in the preceding generations, and the cultural knowledge of Englishmen in Greece, in particular the fame of Lord Byron dying in Greece in 1823 while supporting the struggle for Greek independence from the Ottoman Empire. I am not able to provide a full account of the social history that led to the image Durrell proposed but it is clear that if we view stereotypes as cultural representations then they exist beyond our own personal experiences of others, in the shared culture that we learn from other members of our cultural group.

Cultural stereotypes

We have seen how the limitations of cognition could lead to a biased or stereotypical perception through our interpretation of our experiences (Chapters 2–4). However, much of the book has echoed Lippmann (1922) in arguing that stereotypes are 'given' by the culture as well as 'made' by the person. In this chapter I shall be considering how these are given to us: the cultural transmission of 'common knowledge'. To achieve this I shall focus on the *social representations* theory of Serge Moscovici (1984).

Social representations

Moscovici (1961) examined the communication of psychoanalytic ideas into people's 'everyday' or 'common-sense' explanations of others. He drew his information from the mass media and a questionnaire given to more than 2,000 people in France in the 1950s. His results showed that everyday explanations did employ psychoanalytic ideas and concepts but that different groups of people drew on the theory to different degrees. Also the common-sense representations involved only certain aspects of the theory. When someone explains someone else by saying 'oh, she has a complex about that' or 'he says he hates her but he really still loves her – it's just a defensive reaction' they are using psychoanalytic concepts – although maybe not exactly as Freud proposed – to provide shared understandings of the behaviour of others. Thus:

ideas of revolutionary scope, such as those of Freud or Marx, or artistic movements which sweep away everything in their path, are assimilated by a great many people, leaving a durable impression on their way of thinking, of speaking, of understanding themselves, or of understanding the world in which they live . . . and finally everyone considers them as being independent and forming part of 'reality'. We ourselves see social representations forming, so to speak, before our eyes, in the media, in public places through this process of communication which never happens without some transformation.

(Moscovici, 1998, p. 239)

The importance of the concept of social representations is that it provides a way of explaining everyday knowledge within a cultural group. Moscovici (1998, p. 222) terms them 'intellectual constructions of thought'. Shared understandings or social knowledge are produced within the group through the formation and development of social representations. The Greek image of the British can be seen as a social representation, collectively held within Greek society, learnt and developed through the communication between the members of the social group.

A social representation is a 'system of ideas, values and practices' (Moscovici, 1973, p. xiii) which provides individuals with a way of making sense of people and events in their social world, and it also allows individuals in the social group to communicate with each other as they share these common representations of the people and events in their world (Moscovici, 1973). Consider a person developing a runny nose, a sore throat and feeling exhausted. What does this mean? Is it evil pouring out? Is it a punishment for bad thoughts? We are most likely to talk about this as 'a cold' or 'a viral infection'. Work colleagues will say: 'go home and get to bed'. We believe the cold might spread by the person coughing and sneezing on other people. And often the person will rest for a day or two and take hot lemon and honey to relieve the symptoms. The experience will be represented as a minor illness by present-day society, but notice that 'viral infection' is a fairly modern representation, not used by our Victorian forebears.

In the formation of social representations two processes are important in order to make the unfamiliar familiar: *anchoring* and *objectification* (Moscovici, 1984). Anchoring is the process of naming and classifying the unfamiliar in terms of what is known. Consider the invention of the motor car in the nineteenth century. How can the concept be communicated to others who do not know about it? Referring to it as a 'horseless carriage' links it to something known (everyone knew what a horse-drawn carriage was). Then it is anchored in the known: carriages take people from place to place but this carriage does not require a horse to pull it. Not only is the category of 'carriage' modified to include this new object but through the use of the term we develop a conventional definition of 'car' that is communicated within the social group. Objectification is the process whereby abstract ideas become concrete and seen as 'objective reality'. Throughout the history of scientific endeavour people have proposed concepts to explain various phenomena: such as the ether, electricity or gravity. Now the ether (a substance assumed in the nineteenth century to exist in the space between things) has been dismissed within scientific knowledge and is no longer part of our common-sense knowledge, although you occasionally hear people make reference to it in conversation. Electricity and gravity seem concrete and 'real' and they are part of our everyday knowledge as social representations. Yet our common knowledge of these things is not the same as the scientific understanding of the concepts, as we can find out by asking people to describe what electricity and gravity are. Abstract concepts such as the psychoanalytic terms examined by Moscovici (1961) become modified and objectified in their social representations. In the popular representation some people have larger egos than others and some need to have their egos 'deflated' as they are too big. We understand what someone means when they tell us that their boss has a large ego, due to the social representation of 'ego' (which actually differs from the abstract concept of 'ego' proposed within psychoanalytic theory itself).

Through the processes of anchoring and objectification our common-sense or everyday knowledge is constructed, conventionalized, communicated and reproduced within a society or culture. Social representations form the *consensual universes* (Moscovici, 1984, 1998) within a culture – the agreement on what constitutes the social reality that is common knowledge (or even common-sense knowledge) as opposed to the *reified universe* of abstract or scientific knowledge. Social representations do not have to develop from scientific knowledge: common knowledge about health (Herzlich, 1973) and madness (Jodelet, 1991) have both been investigated as social representations.

Social representations are not explanations at the level of the individual but are essentially social, as they are collectively held by the group, and the social process of social interaction and communication is crucial to their construction. Moscovici (1998) argues that social representations can be viewed as a loosely tied 'network' of ideas, metaphors and images (p. 244). He presents the analogy of money to indicate how social representations are expressed and communicated. They may be represented in different ways (in a newspaper article, in a television show) but we see them as the same, just as a £10 note is the same as two £5 notes. Also, like money, they are not essentially an individual, personal characteristic. If I put a £10 note in a bank, I do not expect them to give me the exact same note when I withdraw it; any £10 coinage will do. Another person will have the specific £10 note I put in the bank. However, there is a personal aspect in that I regard the money in my pocket as mine and the knowledge I communicate as my own. Just as I might give you some of my money, I might communicate some of my (common) knowledge to you.

The people who share social representations make up the social group in Moscovici's terms (Smith and Bond, 1998, p. 303) and social groups are distinguishable from each other by the differences in their everyday knowledge (Flick, 1998). Hewstone *et al.* (1982) showed that boys at selective private schools ('public' schools) and non-selective state schools ('comprehensive' schools) in Britain had very different representations of themselves and the other group. A more recent example from the 1990s has been in the way two horrific shootings were viewed by politicians in

Britain and in the United States of America. When a gunman randomly murdered children in a Scottish school politicians spoke of the danger of guns, and the British government, soon after, tightened the already very strict gun laws. When two young gunmen randomly murdered children in a Denver school United States politicians argued that it was not the availability of guns that was the problem but the anger and violence within some contemporary young people. One Congressman argued that focusing on gun control trivialized the issue (as guns were merely the tools) and there was a need to understand why the people committed the crime.

We should not underestimate the importance of the mass media in the formation and communication of social representations through the rapid communication of ideas and images (Moscovici and Hewstone, 1983; Sommer, 1998). Just as we can infer the social representations employed in a person's conversation, so we can also examine the social representations communicated within media such as newspapers, radio and television. In this book I have endeavoured to describe a number of psychological explanations of stereotypes and stereotyping but it is interesting to consider what the popular social representations of stereotypes and stereotyping are. These are terms frequently used in the media. Next time you hear people use the term on the radio or television see if you can infer how the common-sense use of the term (the social representation) differs from the different psychological perspectives.

Social representations and social cognition

There is a cognitive aspect to Moscovici's theory of social representations. For example, anchoring and objectification are cognitive processes (Potter, 1996) and Moscovici stated that 'social representations are cognitive systems' (Moscovici, 1973, p. xii). But whilst Moscovici accepts there may be links with research in social cognition he also emphasizes differences (Augoustinos and Walker, 1995). In particular, Moscovici (1997) argues that the position adopted in social cognition research, with its focus on the individual and on cognitive processing, lacks the collective and dynamic aspects of cognition. Through social interaction and communication, social knowledge (representations) develops more dynamically within a socio-cultural context than is accepted within 'traditional' social cognition.

Augoustinos and her colleagues have compared social schemas with social representations (Augoustinos and Innes, 1990; Augoustinos and Walker, 1995). Whilst a similarity between them is acknowledged there are also important differences. Social schemas provide an explanation for the way in which a person processes information – influencing expectation and memory, for example. However, this view considers social knowledge to be rather static in that schemas, once formed, are somewhat resistant to change (see Chapter 5). In contrast Moscovici sees social representations as much more 'fluid', in that through interaction and communication they are constantly being renegotiated (Augoustinos and Walker, 1995). Thus, we do not 'discover' social knowledge through our experience of people and events in the social world, but we construct it collectively in a culture, and this is communicated and negotiated between the members of the cultural group. Despite this, the individual perspective of social schemas, with its detailed account of individual cognitive processing, might fruitfully complement the collective perspective of social representations, with its focus on the construction and communication of social knowledge for a fuller understanding of social cognition (Augoustinos and Walker, 1995).

Cultural models

A more culturally sensitive approach to schemas is in the work on *cultural models* (D'Andrade, 1990). D'Andrade defines a cultural model as 'a cognitive schema that is *intersubjectively* shared by a social group' (p. 99, emphasis in the original). The important point here is the acknowledgement that there is a cultural component to a schema. D'Andrade (1990) takes the 'restaurant script' (see Schank and Abelson, 1977) as an example of a cultural model. A script is a schema containing an event sequence. A person's knowledge of what to do in a restaurant is contained in this script. In the restaurant schema there are four components – entering, ordering, eating and leaving – and there are sequences of actions within each component. For example, diners get the menu before ordering the food within the 'ordering' component. However, as D'Andrade (1990) points out, the script is culturally-based in that the type of institution called a 'restaurant' is located in specific cultures. Hence, we can infer that the restaurant script will be different in different cultures. In my (British) restaurant script I expect the waiter/waitress to give all the diners a menu, but this is not necessarily the case in Brazil where only the host might be given the menu to recommend dishes for the guests (Smith and Bond, 1998, p. 50). Similarly, my 'making my bed' script might be to straighten the duvet and cover the bed with the bedspread, but for a Japanese person it might be to fold up the bedding and store it neatly in a cupboard.

Flick (1998) argues that cultural models, whilst being able to account for everyday knowledge within a culture, do not fully deal with the dynamic construction of social knowledge through interaction and communication. Social representations, which explain how everyday knowledge is formed and developed, might be viewed as a way of extending and developing this approach.

Social representations and stereotyping

In discussing Jodelet's (1991) work on the social representations of madness in a French village, Potter (1996) points out: 'It is very important to hold in mind that Jodelet is not trying to find out what mentally ill people are really like – her topic is people's representations, which may be *stereotyped*' (p. 144, my italics). Thus, social knowledge such as the British view of the French will include stereotypical features such as the French being good cooks. The British social representation of the French has not emerged through individual British people observing the French but through the negotiation of a social representation of the French within British culture and through communication between British people concerning the French.

Augoustinos and Walker define a stereotype in terms of social representations:

> stereotypes are more than just cognitive schemas. Stereotypes are social representations: they are objectified cognitive and affective structures about social groups within society which are extensively shared and which emerge and proliferate within the particular social and political milieu of a given historical moment. Stereotypes do not simply exist in individuals' heads. They are socially and discursively constructed in the course of everyday communication, and, once objectified, assume an independent and sometimes prescriptive reality. It is naive to argue that stereotypes are simply a by-product of the cognitive need to simplify reality.
>
> (Augoustinos and Walker, 1995, p. 222)

With stereotypes defined as social representations certain other properties emerge. Social representations have a certain rationality. They are not a product of a failure to think 'properly' or a distortion. Rather they evolve out of the communication within a social group which objectifies and legitimizes the social knowledge of the group (Moscovici, 1997). For example, the stereotype of the Japanese held by students at Princeton University had become more negative between the 1930s and 1950s (Katz and Braly, 1933; Gilbert, 1951). Surely, this change in the representation of the Japanese emerges from the communications within American society within the context of the Japanese as enemies during the Second World War, from the attack on Pearl Harbor onwards. Thus, the actions of the United States in its post-war occupation of Japan and its democratization of the country could be viewed by Americans as legitimate within their understanding of the Japanese and how they should be treated. As we noted in Chapter 4, stereotypes are explanations. They provide a social group with collective explanations as to why different social groups act as they do. The increased negativity of the American stereotype of the Japanese after the

Second World War provided an explanation of the Japanese wartime action in terms of their imputed negative characteristics. So attributions of social behaviour should be considered in terms of the social representations that underlie the explanations (Moscovici and Hewstone, 1983). Indeed, Hewstone and Augoustinos (1998) argue that social representations provide a default explanation prior to careful consideration. These 'automatic explanations' (p. 63) provide the members of a particular cultural group with explanations for a range of circumstances, from why people become ill to why certain social groups are poor.

In an interesting study by Liebes and Katz (1986), a small focus group watched an episode of the American television soap opera *Dallas* which was enormously popular in many countries in the 1980s. Afterwards the group discussed the programme. From the results of a number of small group discussions the researchers showed that different cultural groups interpreted the programme in different ways. When asked about the motivation of the fictional characters, differences were found in the attribution of the source of the motivation. Israeli kibbutz members saw Freudian psychological motives as influencing the different characters; Israeli Arabs saw the individual characters as responsible for their actions; and new Russian immigrants to Israel saw the characters acting according to their social roles, with the particular society responsible for the characters' actions.

Collectivist and individualist cultures

One of the risks of undertaking research within a limited range of cultural groups is that common features may be accepted as universal to all people rather than just the specific cultural groups. A case in point is the fundamental attribution error mentioned in Chapter 4 which suggests that people overestimate the personal over situational factors as a cause of the behaviour of others. However, rather than being 'fundamental' to all people it may be specific to *individualistic* cultures such as those of North America and Europe (e.g. Fletcher and Ward, 1988).

In an *individualistic* culture the individual is regarded primarily as an independent agent within the culture, seeking to obtain their own goals, whereas in a *collectivist* culture the individual is seen as interdependent with other members of the culture, seeking to achieve the goals of the group, such as nation, family or work group (Morales *et al.*, 1998). Hofstede (1980) reported the results of large-scale surveys he had undertaken with employees of IBM in forty different countries concerning work-related values. He found that the collectivist–individualist dimension was an important one for differentiating between the different countries. The key questions for this dimension were: *How important is it to you to have a job that leaves you sufficient time for your personal and family life?* and *How important is it to you to have considerable freedom to adapt your own approach to the job?* Certain countries, typically from North America and Europe, replied that these were very important, indicating individualistic cultures. Examples were the United States of America, Australia, Great Britain and the Netherlands. The replies of another group of countries, mostly from Asia and South America, showed a more collectivistic culture. Examples were Guatemala, Ecuador, Indonesia and Taiwan.

The individualist/collectivist distinction can have important implications for the understanding of people and events. As we saw in Chapter 5, Hinkle and Brown (1990) showed that identification with one's social group is greater for collectivist groups. Also, different cultures will have different social representations: their everyday knowledge of, and explanations for, social behaviour may be quite different. The successful American television soap opera *Dallas* (see above) was not popular in Japan, a more collectivistic society. In a study to examine reasons for this, Katz *et al.* (1991) showed an episode to a small group of Japanese people, and this was followed by a group discussion of the programme. They found that the Japanese focused on the inconsistencies in the programme. For example, even though the programme was about a family they did not behave with love or sympathy towards each other. Katz *et al.* suggest that for the Japanese these inconsistencies did not marry with their expectations of either a television programme or life and hence did not make sense, whereas for

Americans the inconsistencies provided an attractive 'experimental' approach to modern society.

Oyserman and Markus (1998) suggest that individualism and collectivism are different social representations, one focusing on the individual development and the other on the development of the group. With different representations within individualistic and collectivistic cultures it can be argued that attempting to change stereotypes will be more effective when targeted at the individual in an individualistic culture and at the group within a collectivistic culture (Worchel and Rothgerber, 1997).

Media, culture and stereotypes

As mentioned above, Moscovici stresses the involvement of the mass media in the development and maintenance of social representations (Moscovici and Hewstone, 1983). The development of radio, film, television, and the Internet has provided new media for communication, both widening the range of sources as well as speeding up the communication process. Indeed we may even be able to refer to Internet communities where physically separated individuals identify with a group of people communicating over the Internet (e.g. Porter, 1997).

Sommer (1998) provides an example of how television can be involved in the propagation of a social representation. The nihilistic youth style referred to as 'punk' developed in the late 1970s in Britain, with its fashion typified by safety pins and Mohican haircuts and its music exemplified by the Sex Pistols. Sommer argues that presenting this representation through television as a form of rebellious youth (expressing the attitude 'we don't care') helped to anchor and objectify the representation into common, everyday knowledge. Thus, the punk stereotype could be employed with reference to certain young people in other countries. Also, as the representation exists within everyday understanding this allows it to be used to anchor other representations. A certain fashion style might be referred to as 'chic-punk' or 'gothic-punk' in an attempt to explain the particular styles.

We do have to be careful, however, in assuming that the communication between cultures via electronic media will lead to the development of a common social representation. Just as cross-cultural communication can be fraught with misunderstanding (e.g. Smith and Bond, 1998) we must also be aware that the same television programme will not necessarily be interpreted in the same way by people in different cultures (such as in the example of *Dallas*, mentioned above). We should not allow the representation of the 'global village' to blinker us to cultural diversity.

Conclusion

Social representations theory is an interesting theory in terms of this book as it provides us with answers to how common knowledge (including stereotypes) is communicated within a culture. As we saw earlier, it has links to the cognitive approach but emphasizes the importance of knowledge being developed through interpersonal communication rather than simply being 'out there' for a perceiver to process. This interpersonal constructive process of knowledge generation also has echoes in the approach adopted by discourse analysts (Harré, 1998). As Potter and Wetherell (1998) show, social representations theory shares with discourse analysis a move away from the traditional emphasis on cognitive processing to a focus on the cultural contents of social activity, on the importance of interpersonal communication and on social construction. There is also a relationship between social representations and social identity. Social representations establish the common knowledge within a group and hence distinguish the group from others. More specifically, social representations can constrain the scope for ingroup favouritism. As Breakwell (1993) points out, the British representation of the French as better cooks means that this is not a dimension on which British people would claim a superiority. From these different links between social representations and the other approaches to stereotyping it appears that some fruitful integration of approaches is possible.

However, social representations theory has a difficulty with the definition of a group (Potter, 1996). Groups are defined within the theory by common social representations. However, this means that we cannot select a group in order to study its representations without knowing the representations it holds. If we select a group defined outside of representations theory, such as 'the British' or 'accountants', then we may be making the assumption that these are groups that must have common social representations. This also leads us to a problem of the agreement of a representation within and between groups. How do we deal with the variability of the representations held by people within a group? For example, British Labour and Conservative voters may have different representations of being British. Even within the Labour voters there may be a range of differences, so at what point do we define the group with consensus in its social representations?

Summary

Social representations theory argues that common knowledge is constructed through a process of interpersonal communication. Through the processes of anchoring and objectification new representations are developed and become 'everyday knowledge'. Stereotypes can be viewed as social representations and reflect the common-sense view of the group that is communicated between its members. Different cultural groups will differ in the social representations they hold and in the explanations contained within them. In the development of stereotypes, as with all social representations, we should look to all forms of interpersonal communication such as television, books and films in studying their formation and development.

Further reading

Breakwell, G. and Canter, D. (eds) (1993) *Empirical approaches to social representations*. Oxford: Oxford University Press. This looks at how social representations theory has been investigated.

Flick, U. (ed.) (1998) *The psychology of the social*. Cambridge: Cambridge University Press. An advanced set of readings with an excellent chapter by Moscovici (Chapter 14).

Chapter 8

Conclusion

Stereotypes and levels of explanation

S TEREOTYPES ARE AN IMPORTANT concept in social psychology. Not surprisingly, given this importance, attempts to explain why and how they arise have come from a number of different theoretical positions, as we have seen in this book: from being viewed as a feature of an evolutionarily functional prejudgement of the 'unfinished mind', to the result of the nature of cognitive processing and intergroup perception, to social representations and subject-positions within discourse. Rather than regarding this as an indication that we still do not know what stereotypes are, we can consider how the interplay between the ideas has developed our understanding of the subject.

The theories of the 1950s tended to view stereotyping as indicating either a prejudiced person (such as the authoritarian personality) or a mental weakness (such as faulty thinking that should be stopped). This indicated two types of people in society – those who thought in a rigid stereotyped way and those who did not – with the experts (the psychologists) firmly in the latter camp. However, new research showed that prejudiced thinking was not more rigid than unprejudiced thinking (Billig, 1985), and that all people might be influenced in their thinking by the nature of human cognition (e.g. Tajfel, 1969; Hamilton, 1979). But in developing an explanation that gave primacy to mental processing two important aspects of stereotyping tended to be ignored. First, knowledge may be constructed through social interaction and negotiation, and, second, we exist as members of groups in societies and cultures with our own cultural understandings and meanings of people and events. By emphasizing one aspect of stereotyping we must be careful that we are not excluding another.

Rather than contrasting the explanations, we can consider them in terms of different levels of explanation (Hewstone, 1997).

Different approaches will not only imply different methods of analysis but will also seek an explanation of stereotyping at a particular level. Levels can range from those concerning mechanisms within the person to the social and cultural. Identifying a stereotype as a schema or prototype is seeking an explanation in terms of the individual person and the processes operating within them. It is not surprising that explanations at this level have a focus on the limitations of human information processing. We can also consider the interpersonal level where explanations are sought in the relationships between people in different situations, and explain, say, a woman relating to a young man in different situations in terms of mother–son or boss–employee relationship. At a more social level we can explain psychological findings in terms of group membership. As we saw in Chapter 5, a person may act and perceive themselves *as a doctor* rather than as an individual. We can even go on to a cultural or ideological level where ideological positions are seen as the focus of explanation. We might be able to draw out ideological positions contained within discourse or, indeed, examine the social representations that are accepted as common knowledge within a culture. The different understandings of people within individualist and collectivist cultures can be explained at this level. Overall, we may find that one level alone is simply not adequate to explain the nature of stereotyping.

'Rotten apples', 'canteen culture' and institutionalized racism

We can see the practical importance of understanding stereotyping at different levels of explanation in the MacPherson report on the police investigation into the murder of the black teenager Stephen Lawrence (MacPherson, 1999). In 1993 in South London two young men, Stephen Lawrence and Duwayne Brooks, were waiting for a bus on their way home when they were attacked by a group of five young white men who stabbed Stephen Lawrence to death. The only possible explanation was that this had been a wholly unprovoked attack by a group of racist murderers. Despite a group of suspects being identified, three of whom were tried and acquitted, no one was convicted for the crime. Stephen Lawrence was only 18 and had been looking forward to training to be an architect. An inquiry headed by Sir William MacPherson was set up by the Government in July 1997 at the request of Stephen Lawrence's parents to look into the police investigation of the case. The inquiry focused on the failure of the police investigations and on the question of racism within the Metropolitan Police service.

It is not my aim to go into the details of the case but I would like to focus on the stereotyping of black people by the police, highlighted in the report, to illustrate some of the research that has been considered in this book. First, there was the treatment of the key witness Duwayne Brooks. It was noted in the report that individual police officers treated Duwayne Brooks in terms of their negative stereotype of a young black man, commenting on one officer's 'racist stereotypical behaviour at the scene. He assumed that there had been a fight. He wholly failed to assess Duwayne Brooks as a primary victim. He failed thus to take advantage of the help which Mr Brooks could have given' (paragraph 46.28i), and 'Mr Brooks was by some officers sidelined and ignored, because of racist stereotyping particularly at the scene and the hospital. He was never properly treated as a victim' (46.28iv). The report points out that 'no officer dealt properly at the scene with Mr Brooks' and states:

> We are driven to the conclusion that Mr Brooks was stereotyped as a young black man exhibiting unpleasant hostility and agitation, who could not be expected to help, and whose condition and status simply did not need further examination or understanding. We believe that Mr Brooks' colour and such stereotyping played their part in the collective failure of those involved to treat him properly and according to his needs.
>
> (5.12)

This is further emphasized after an account of a police officer's description of Mr Brooks. 'We do not believe that a young white man in a similar position would have been dealt with in the same way. He was simply not treated professionally and appropriately and according to his needs' (5.31).

So was this just a small group of racist police officers? We could argue that all organizations have their 'bad apples' and unfortunately these were involved here. The report is categorical in stating that this is not the case, quoting the Police Commissioner: 'Racism in the police is much more than "bad apples". Racism as you have pointed out, can occur through a lack of care and a lack of understanding' (6.25). The report draws on the concepts of 'unwitting', 'unconscious' and 'unintentional' racism (6.12) in capturing the nature of the racism involved. Thus, the report identified a widespread 'unwitting racism' resulting in part from the 'racist stereotyping of black people as potential criminals or troublemakers' (6.17).

This poses a question: if the police were not intentionally racist, and presumably as police officers they wished to solve crimes, why would they treat Mr Brooks in a way that did not help the proper investigation of the murder? The answer appears to lie in much of the research considered in this book. If stereotypes are common knowledge, that is, commonly held views within a group, then the group members will tend to hold these views as their 'knowledge' of the people and events. But why would this particular stereotype arise within the police? The predominantly white police, unfamiliar with minority ethnic communities (6.17) may then only 'meet members of the black community in confrontational situations' (6.27, also 37.18). Thus, white police officers primarily experience black people in the restricted setting of potential crime. As we saw in Chapters 2 and 3, both the categorization and the limited experience of the white police in meeting black members of the community could have led to an illusory correlation of black people and crime. However, note that this bears no association with *actual* criminal activity and we can see that the association arises from the institutional structure and organization of the police (its members, its working practices and its occupational culture), producing these restricted encounters of white police officers and black people. In part these are the features that led the report to argue that institutional racism existed within the police service (6.45).

Does not the evidence inform the police officers that the stereotype is wrong? We can see from Chapters 3 and 4 that this may not happen. If the information is dealt with heuristically then it may be processed and remembered in terms of the stereotype. Furthermore, new information may be interpreted and explained in terms of the stereotype by making stereotypical attributions. In terms of the cognitive explanations in the earlier part of this book we can see that Mr Brooks was not categorized as a 'victim' or 'witness' but as a 'young black man' and then described as 'agitated', 'aggressive' and 'virtually uncontrollable' (5.10). Notice that these descriptions, even if correct, were not then *attributed to the situation* – anyone would be suffering terrible trauma at the murder of a friend – but were *attributed stereotypically* to the person – the 'hostility' of a young black man. A second example cited in the report is of a 'female white police officer on seeing a black person driving a very nice car just said "I wonder who he robbed to get that?", and then she realised that she was actually voicing an unconscious assumption' (6.11). This may then have an effect on behaviour, with a greater proportion of black people being stopped and searched than white people (37.18, 45.8).

We have seen in both Chapter 5 and Chapter 7 that common representations are held within a social group. The police are often referred to as having a 'canteen culture' (6.17, 37.24) where there is both a strong sense of social identity and a place for sharing views. Here, specific social representations (the police views on black people) would be communicated to new police officers. Within a tightly knit 'canteen culture' the finding of consensus amongst the ingroup members (the police) on the perception of an outgroup (black people) can lead to an individual member believing that their view is validated and is 'common knowledge'. Furthermore, through social comparison processes (Chapter 5), the ingroup will also endeavour to enhance their social identity through ingroup favouritism and thus view outgroup members as inferior. Thus, both group processes and cultural differences create a gulf between the groups.

A final point, drawing on Chapter 6, is the way race is discussed by all those involved, including myself in this book. What are the story lines being developed? What arguments are being proposed? For example, we can analyse the discourse between the Police Commissioner and the inquiry around 'institutionalized racism' by considering the arguments involved. Also, like Potter and Wetherell's (1987) work describing white New Zealanders' discussions of Maoris, we can examine the different police officers' accounts of the black participants within the case, described in the report. For example, what is the function of the discourse of one officer who 'accepted that the individuals involved [in the attack] were racist and that there was a "degree of racism" involved but insisted that he could not convince himself that racism was the only reason for the attack on Stephen Lawrence' (24.20)? We can also analyse the report itself as a text and examine its structure and organization and the language it employs.

Each of the different explanations considered in this book offers some account of the stereotyping that may be pertinent to this case. But, rather than the theoretical issues discussed in this book, the report focused on the practical failings in bringing murderers to justice. Seventy recommendations were made by the inquiry as an outcome of their investigations. In terms of changing the stereotype of black people held by the police there were a number of initiatives, which we can link to different levels in explaining stereotyping. A campaign was undertaken within the Metropolitan Police service to change the stereotype of black people held by the police. One example is a poster with the question, 'What do you call a black man in a BMW?' followed by the answer: 'A police sergeant in a patrol car.' This can be seen as an attempt to get individual police officers to question the views they hold. As we saw in Chapter 4, counter-stereotypical information can change stereotypes, but only in certain circumstances. The research discussed in that chapter indicates that there is a risk that black police officers will be subtyped and the stereotype of black people held by the police will not change. However, diffused counter-stereotypical information has a greater effect on stereotype change, so greater numbers of black police officers could result in stereotype change. Indeed, the Home Secretary demanded an increase in the recruitment of the police from ethnic minority groups (*The Times*, 10 February 1999), in part to help change the canteen culture of the police.

Interestingly, more black police officers should then provide a crossing of the predominantly white category of 'police' with a racial mix, which, from Chapter 5, could lead to a reduction in prejudice. Also, if the encounters of the police with black people were widened and stop-and-search practices had a more appropriate ethnic balance then the illusory correlation between black people and 'potential criminal' would not develop in the minds of new police officers (see Chapter 3).

Clearly, we should not ignore the wide-ranging institutional changes recommended in the report and indeed be very clear that a brief psychological analysis such as this is merely able to examine a small part of a complex issue. For example, the central question of institutional relationships may be better understood through a sociological analysis (Holdaway, 1999). Yet wider changes in society might lead to cultural change in the development of new social representations and in certain subject-positions within discourse becoming no longer acceptable.

Conclusion

We have seen that much of the psychological research on stereotyping has focused on how we make sense of the world around us and how the nature of human cognition may result in stereotypical judgements. Yet even those researchers who have generated a focus on cognition (such as Lippmann or Tajfel) also acknowledge the importance of culture in the contents of the stereotypes we hold. It is through a consideration of both cognition and culture that we will gain a better understanding of stereotyping.

Stereotyping is both a central topic in social psychology and a problem. It is intimately linked to our everyday understanding of people and events but also intimately linked to prejudice and discrimination. To what extent are we all condemned by the nature of human cognition to perceive in a stereotypical manner? How much do our explanations and sense of identity rely on making discriminations between ingroups and outgroups? We must be careful that in providing an explanation for some aspects of stereotyping we are not ignoring others. In examining the role of cognition in stereotyping we should not underestimate the importance of culture to stereotyping, nor should we limit our understanding through the arguments we construct to explain it.

Further reading

Brown, R. (1995) *Prejudice – its social psychology*. Oxford: Blackwell. This is a clearly-written, 'traditional' account of the psychology of prejudice.

Potter, J. and Wetherell, M. (1998) 'Social representations, discourse analysis and racism', in U. Flick (ed.) *The psychology of the social*. Cambridge: Cambridge University Press. This chapter provides a discourse-analytic interpretation of racism as well as critiquing the social representations approach.

Glossary

anchoring In social representations theory associating new information to something known.

attribution The process of deciding on the cause of a particular act carried out by a person.

authoritarianism A personality characteristic, proposed by Adorno *et al.* (1950), associated with prejudice.

automatic processing Human information processing that takes place without requiring attention. It is seen as developing through practice and operates in a fast, unconscious, inflexible and unintentional manner.

base-rate The underlying statistical probabilities associated with a particular event.

categorization Assigning an object, person or event to a particular category.

cognitive busyness A person is said to be cognitively busy when they are undertaking a cognitive task (such as remembering a long number) requiring conscious attention.

cognitive complexity The number of concepts or constructs a person employs in their representations of people and events.

cognitive load The cognitive tasks a person is performing currently (such as remembering a number).

cognitive miser The model of the person that assumes we are 'miserly' in the use of our limited capacity processing resources. Due to our limitations in information processing capacity we employ strategies to deal with the information processing demands upon us in order to solve problems quickly and adequately rather than following logical or statistical methods.

collectivism A characteristic of a group and its members where there is an emphasis on cooperative actions for the collective achievement of the group rather than individual achievement. Individual group members are seen to be interdependent. Used in reference to certain cultural groups.

contact hypothesis The hypothesis that the members of one group will have a more realistic perception (i.e. less prejudiced) of another group if they come into contact with its members.

controlled attention See conscious attention.

correspondent inference Associating the behaviour of a person to their personality rather than to the situation.

crossed categories Two categories cross where a set of people can be categorized differently on the two categories. If categorized on one characteristic (say, men and women) different people will be in the two groups compared to when they are categorized on the second characteristic (say, southerners and northerners).

conscious attention The employment of limited capacity information processing resources. Conscious attention takes time and we are limited in what we can deal with. However, novel information can be dealt with and information can be processed flexibly. A thoughtful consideration of a problem is associated with conscious attention.

cultural model A form of cognitive schema that is shared amongst the members of a cultural group. For example, an understanding of what happens in a restaurant can be seen as a cultural model as a 'restaurant' has a cultural definition and different cultures may have different models of both what a restaurant is and the sequence of events that takes place within it.

cultural stereotype A stereotype that is shared by the members of a particular culture.

deduction A reasoning process where a general rule is applied to a specific instance: for example, from the rule 'all people have lungs' we can deduce that Susan standing before us has lungs.

depersonalization Perceiving oneself as a category member rather than as a unique individual.

discourse All forms of spoken and written 'texts'. An informal conversation or a written text are examples of discourse.

discourse analysis The analysis of discourse. Psychologists undertaking discourse analysis seek to draw out the various ways in which people and events are constructed within discourse and the functions that these constructions serve.

expectancy violation Expectancy violation occurs when we learn information about a person that goes against our expectation of them based on their group membership.

exemplar A typical member of a category. An apple is an exemplar of a fruit.

Gestalt An overall, organized structure. Used in terms of perception it refers to the global aspect of a perception where 'the whole is greater than the sum of the parts'.

heuristic A 'rule of thumb'. A strategy. It is argued by social cognition theorists that, due to our limited processing capacity, many of our judgements concerning other people are based on heuristics rather than logical or statistical reasoning.

illusory correlation A belief that two things are correlated (such as criminality and a particular social group) when they are not.

implicit personality theory A person's beliefs concerning the association of, and interrelationship between, personality characteristics.

individualism A characteristic of a group and its members that emphasizes individual achievement over that of the group. Individual group members are seen to be independent of each other. Used to refer to certain cultural groups.

induction A reasoning process by which specific examples are used to infer a general rule: for example, each of the dogs I have encountered has fur so I induce that all dogs have fur.

ingroup A group of which the perceiver (the person making a judgement) is a member.

interpretative repertoire A common theme that a discourse analyst has drawn out of their analysis of discourse.

limited capacity processing Information processing associated with conscious attention.

mental model   A cognitive representation of a person, object or event that guides our understanding of it.

noncommon effects   Two potential causes for a person's action may have a number of common effects. The noncommon effects are the effects that result from one of the potential causes but not the other.

normative fit   The degree to which a particular categorization fits the situation in terms of the social meanings of the people involved. The category 'parent' is a better normative fit than 'doctor' when a woman doctor is visiting a school to see the teachers about her child.

objectification   In social representations theory, objectification is the process by which a new representation becomes 'concrete' and achieves an 'objective' reality to the members of the social group holding the representation.

outgroup   A group of which the perceiver (the person making a judgement) is not a member.

particularization   A person can be categorized in a number of ways. When a person is arguing their viewpoint they will choose a particular category in which to place a person. A particularization will be used within an argument to support a particular ideological position.

personal construct   According to personal construct theory, in learning to make sense of people and events we develop a set of personal constructs. Each construct (such as happy–sad, friend–enemy) is employed to make sense of a particular situation.

personal identity   A sense of identity focusing on personal, individual characteristics rather than group membership.

personal stereotype   A stereotype developed and employed by an individual rather than by members of a social group.

prime   If the response to a stimulus is influenced by a preceding stimulus the first stimulus is said to 'prime' the second. For example, people are quicker to recognize the word 'doctor' if it has been primed by the word 'nurse'.

prototype   A mental representation of a person or an object containing the typical characteristics of it. For example, your prototype of a chair will be a 'model' of what you regard as a typical chair.

relational   A relational group is one where the group members are concerned about their position relative to other comparison groups (such as supporters of a particular football team in a league). The opposite is an autonomous group.

rhetoric   Traditionally the art of using language persuasively. In Billig's (1987) work it is proposed that thought can be understood through the arguments employed in people's public discourse. In taking a rhetorical approach to thought we can examine the arguments employed by both prejudiced and unprejudiced people.

role   A role is a social position such as doctor or mother. Within a social group there will be a particular set of expectations about the behaviour of a person inhabiting the role (in-role behaviour) such as a doctor treating the sick and a mother caring for her child.

salience   A certain characteristic of an object or a person which stands out in a particular context is said to be salient. We will attend to a salient characteristic. Context influences salience, with the unusual or odd attracting our attention. If there is only one man in a group of women then 'gender' will be seen to be salient in this context.

schemas   Schemas are an important concept in social cognition. Schemas are knowledge structures that organize our knowledge about an object, person or event. Thus, my 'nurse' schema is the organized knowledge about nurses, including both characteristics of 'nurse' (e.g. caring) and expectations about how they will behave in certain circumstances (e.g. help a child who has fallen over).

social constructionism   The psychological perspective that proposes that human psychology is 'constructed' within interaction and through language rather than being determined by biological and environmental causes.

social conventions   Within a culture there are certain 'rules' of conduct, such as shaking hands on greeting. People from different cultures may have different social conventions. In deciding why someone did not follow a social convention it is a question of whether we attribute the cause to a lack of knowledge of the convention or to a deliberate flouting of it.

social identity   The sense of identity we gain through being a member of a social group.

social cognition   An approach to social psychology that focuses on cognitive explanations of social experience and investigates the nature of cognitive processing. In this approach concepts such as 'schemas' are used to explain how and why the social perceiver interprets the world as they do.

social representation   A social representation is a representation of people or events in the social world (including values, ideas and practices) that is held by members of a particular social group. This social representation is not only 'common knowledge' but allows for communication between group members on the basis of the shared understanding of the person or event.

social stereotype   A social stereotype is one that is shared by the members of a particular social group.

stereotype   A category of people is assigned a set of common characteristics which define the stereotyped view of this group. When a person is identified as a member of this group they are then attributed the stereotypical characteristics. Thus, all group members are placed in the 'strait-jacket' of the stereotype. It has been proposed that a stereotype is a type of schema, prototype or social representation.

stereotype-consistent information   Information that is consistent with a stereotype, such as learning that a lawyer (stereotypically 'ambitious') has applied to a prestigious law firm.

stereotype-inconsistent information   Information that is inconsistent with a stereotype, such as learning that an artist (stereotypically 'poor at mathematics') showed the scientist the flaw in his calculations.

Subject-position   A position taken up within a discourse. In discussing an essay with a student a lecturer may take up the subject-position of 'expert'.

subtyping   In explaining why a particular group member or members did not behave in a stereotypical manner a perceiver might subtype this subset as a subcategory of the original group. In this way the stereotype of the group is maintained for the majority of group members with the subgroup as the exception. For example, on discovering an artistic engineer a perceiver might subtype this person as 'a polymath engineer' - good at everything. An artistic engineer is seen as an exception ('there are some people who are good at everything') and the stereotype of 'normal or typical' engineers as not artistic is maintained.

trait   A personality characteristic.

References

Adorno, T.W., Frenkel-Brunswick, E., Levison, D.J. and Stanford, R.N. (1950) *The authoritarian personality*. New York: Harper & Row.

Allport, G.W. (1954) *The nature of prejudice*. Cambridge: Addison-Wesley.

Anastasio, P., Bachman, B., Gaertner, S. and Dovidio, J. (1997) 'Categorization, recategorization and common ingroup identity', in R. Spears, P.J. Oakes, N. Ellemers and S.A. Haslam (eds) *The social psychology of stereotyping and group life*. Oxford: Blackwell.

Andersen, S.M., Klatzky, R.L. and Murray, J. (1990) 'Traits and social stereotypes: efficiency differences in social information processing', *Journal of Personality and Social Psychology*, 59, 192–201.

Anderson, N.H. (1965) 'Averaging versus adding as a stimulus-combination rule in impression formation', *Journal of Experimental Psychology*, 70, 394–400.

Antaki, C. (1988) 'Explanations, communication and social cognition', in C. Antaki (ed.) *Analysing everyday explanations: a casebook of methods*. London: Sage.

Asch, S.E. (1946) 'Forming impression of personality', *Journal of Abnormal and Social Psychology*, 41, 258–290.

Asch, S.E. (1956) 'Studies of independence and conformity: a minority of one against a unanimous majority', *Psychological Monographs*, 70, No. 9 (Whole No. 416).

Asch, S.E. and Zukier, H. (1984) 'Thinking about persons', *Journal of Personality and Social Psychology*, 46, 1230–1240.

Augoustinos, M. and Innes, J.M. (1990) 'Towards an integration of social representations and social schema theory', *British Journal of Social Psychology*, 29, 213–231.

Augoustinos, M. and Walker, I. (1995) *Social cognition: an integrated introduction*. London: Sage.

Banaji, M.R., Hardin, C. and Rothman, A.J. (1993) 'Implicit stereotyping in person judgement', *Journal of Personality and Social Psychology*, 65, 272–281.

Bargh, J.A., Chen, M., and Burrows, L. (1996) 'Automaticity of social behaviour: direct effects of trait construct and stereotype activation on action', *Journal of Personality and Social Psychology*, 71, 230–244.

Bartlett, F.C. (1932) *Remembering: a study in experimental and social psychology*. Cambridge: Cambridge University Press.

Berry, D.S. and McArthur, L.Z. (1986) 'Perceiving character in faces: the impact of age-related craniofacial changes on social perception', *Psychological Bulletin*, 100, 3–18.

Berscheid, E. (1985) 'Interpersonal attraction', in G. Lindzey and E. Aronson (eds) *Handbook of social psychology*. New York: Random House.

Bettencourt, B.A., Dill, K.E., Greathouse, S.A., Charlton, K. and Mulholland, A. (1997) 'Evaluations of ingroup and outgroup members: the role of category-based expectancy violation', *Journal of Experimental Social Psychology*, 33, 244–275.

Bieri, J. (1955) 'Cognitive complexity – simplicity and predictive behaviour', *Journal of Abnormal and Social Psychology*, 51, 263–8.

Billig, M. (1985) 'Prejudice, categorization and particularization: from a perceptual to a rhetorical approach', *European Journal of Social Psychology*, 15, 79–103.

Billig, M. (1987) *Arguing and thinking: a rhetorical approach to social psychology.* Cambridge: Cambridge University Press.
Billig, M. and Tajfel, H. (1973) 'Social categorization and similarity in intergroup behaviour', *European Journal of Social Psychology*, 3, 37–52.
Bodenhausen, G.V. (1990) 'Second-guessing the jury: stereotypic and hindsight biases in perceptions of court cases', *Journal of Applied Social Psychology*, 20, 1112–1121.
Bodenhausen, G.V. and Wyer, R.S. Jr. (1985) 'Effects of stereotypes on decision making and information-processing strategies', *Journal of Personality and Social Psychology*, 48, 267–282.
Breakwell, G.M. (1993) 'Integrating paradigms, methodological implications', in G.M. Breakwell and D.V. Canter (eds) *Empirical approaches to social representations.* Oxford: Clarendon.
Brigham, J.C. (1971) 'Ethnic stereotypes', *Psychological Bulletin*, 76, 15–38.
Broadbent, D.E. (1958) *Perception and communication.* Oxford: Pergamon.
Brown, R. (1965) *Social psychology.* London: Collier-Macmillan.
Brown, R. (1995) *Prejudice – its social psychology.* Oxford: Blackwell.
Brown, R.J., Hinkle, S., Ely, P.G., Fox-Cardamone, L., Maras, P. and Taylor, L.A. (1992) 'Recognising group diversity: individualist-collectivist and autonomous-relational social orientations and their implications for intergroup processes', *British Journal of Social Psychology*, 31, 327–342.
Brunas-Wagstaff, J. (1998) *Personality: a cognitive approach.* London: Routledge.
Bruner, J.S. (1957) 'On perceptual readiness', *Psychological Review*, 64, 123–152.
Bruner, J.S. (1973) *Beyond the information given: studies in the psychology of knowing.* New York: Norton.
Bruner, J.S. and Tagiuri, R. (1954) 'The perception of people', in G. Lindzay (ed.) *Handbook of social psychology*, volume 2, Cambridge, Mass.: Addison-Wesley.
Bruner, J.S., Goodnow, J.J. and Austin, J.G. (1956) *A study of thinking.* New York: Wiley.
Burman, E. and Parker, I. (1993) 'Introduction – discourse analysis: the turn to the text', in E. Burman and I. Parker (eds) *Discourse analytic research – repertoires and readings of texts in action.* London: Routledge.

Burr, V. (1995) *An introduction to social constructionism*. London: Routledge.

Burr, V. (1998) *Gender and social psychology*. London: Routledge.

Campbell, D.T. (1967) 'Stereotypes and the perception of group differences', *American Psychologist*, 22, 817–829.

Cantor, N. and Mischel, W. (1977) 'Traits as prototypes: effects on recognition memory', *Journal of Personality and Social Psychology*, 35, 38–48.

Cantor, N. and Mischel, W. (1979) 'Prototypes in person perception', in L. Berkowitz (ed.) *Advances in experimental social psychology*, vol. 12. New York: Academic Press.

Casselden, P.A. and Hampson, S.E. (1990) 'Forming impressions from incongruent traits', *Journal of Personality and Social Psychology*, 59, 253–262.

Cauthern, N.R., Robinson, I.E. and Krauss, H.H. (1971) 'Stereotypes: a review of the literature 1926–1968', *Journal of Social Psychology*, 84, 103–125.

Chaiken, S. and Trope, V. (eds) (1999) *Dual-process theories in social psychology*. New York: Guilford Press.

Chaiken, S., Liberman, A. and Eagly, A.H. (1989) 'Heuristic and systematic information processing within and beyond the persuasion context', In J.S. Uleman and J.A. Bargh (eds) *Unintended thought: limits of awareness, intention and control*. New York: Guilford Press.

Chapman, K.L., Leonard, L.B. and Mervis, C.B. (1986) 'The effect of feedback on young children's inappropriate word usage', *Journal of Child Language*, 13, 101–117.

Cherry, E.C. (1953) 'Some experiments on the recognition of speech, with one and with two ears', *Journal of the Acoustic Society of America*, 25, 975–979.

Clark, E.V. (1993) *The lexicon in acquisition*. Cambridge: Cambridge University Press.

Collins, A.M. and Quillian, M.R. (1969) 'Retrieval time from semantic memory', *Journal of Verbal Learning and Verbal Behaviour*, 8, 240–248.

Crossman, E.R.F.W. (1953) 'Entropy and choice time: the effect of frequency unbalance on choice-response', *Quarterly Journal of Experimental Psychology*, 5, 41–51.

D'Andrade, R. (1990) 'Some propositions about the relations between culture and human cognition', in J. Stigler, R. Shweder and G.

Herdt (eds) *Cultural psychology – essays on comparative human development*. Cambridge: Cambridge University Press.

Davies, B. and Harré, R. (1990) 'Positioning: the discursive production of selves', *Journal for the Theory of Social Behaviour*, 20, 43–63.

Deaux, K. (1976) *The behaviour of women and men*. Monterey, Calif.: Brooks/Cole.

Deschamps, J.-C. and Devos, T. (1998) 'Regarding the relationship between social identity and personal identity', in S. Worchel, J.F. Morales, D. Páez and J.-C. Deschamps (eds) *Social identity – international perspectives*. London: Sage.

Deschamps, J.-C. and Doise, W. (1978) 'Crossed category memberships in intergroup relations', in H. Tajfel (ed.) *Differentiation between social groups*. London: Academic Press.

Deutsch, M. and Gerard, H.B. (1955) 'A study of normative and informational influence upon individual judgement', *Journal of Abnormal and Social Psychology*, 51, 629–636.

Devine, P.G. (1989) 'Stereotypes and prejudice: their automatic and controlled components', *Journal of Personality and Social Psychology*, 56, 5–18.

Devine, P.G. and Sherman, S.J. (1992) 'Intuitive versus rational judgment and the role of stereotyping in the human condition: Kirk or Spock?', *Psychological Inquiry*, 3, 153–159.

Dijksterhuis, A. and van Knippenberg, A. (1995) 'Memory for stereotype-consistent and stereotype-inconsistent information as a function of processing pace', *European Journal of Social Psychology*, 25, 689–693.

Dijksterhuis, A., Spears, R., Postmes, T., Stapel, D.A., Koomen, W., van Knippenberg, A. and Scheepers, D. (1998) 'Seeing one thing and doing another: contrast effects in automatic behaviour', *Journal of Personality and Social Psychology*, 75, 862–871.

Dion, K., Berscheid, E. and Walster, E. (1972) 'What is beautiful is good', *Journal of Personality and Social Psychology*, 24, 285–290.

Dollard, J., Doob, L.W., Miller Jr., N.E., Mowrer, O.H. and Sears, R.R. (1939) *Frustration and aggression*. New Haven, Conn.: Yale University Press.

Dovidio, J.F., Gaertner, S.L., Validzic, A., Matoka, K., Johnson, B. and Frazier, S. (1997a) 'Extending the benefits of recategorization: evaluations, self-disclosure, and helping', *Journal of Experimental Social Psychology*, 33, 401–420.

Dovidio, J.F., Kawakami, K., Johnson, C., Johnson, B. and Howard, A. (1997b) 'On the nature of prejudice: automatic and controlled processes', *Journal of Experimental Social Psychology*, 33, 510–540.

Durrell, L. (1957) *Bitter Lemons*. London: Faber and Faber.

Eagly, A.H. and Steffen, V.J. (1984) 'Gender stereotypes stem from the distribution of women and men into social roles', *Journal of Personality and Social Psychology*, 46, 735–754.

Edwards, D. (1996) *Discourse and cognition*. London: Sage.

Edwards, D. and Potter, J. (1992) *Discursive psychology*. London: Sage.

Eimas, P.D., Siqueland, E.R., Jusczyk, P. and Vigorito, J. (1971) 'Speech perception in infants', *Science*, 171, 303–306.

Fischhoff, B. and Bar-Hillel, M. (1984) 'Diagnosticity and the baserate effect', *Memory and Cognition*, 12, 402–410.

Fiske, S.T. (1992a) 'Stereotypes work . . . but only sometimes: comment on how to motivate the "unfinished mind"', *Psychological Inquiry*, 3, 161–162.

Fiske, S.T. (1992b) 'Thinking is for doing: portraits of social cognition from daguerreotype to laserphoto', *Journal of Personality and Social Psychology*, 63, 877–889.

Fiske, S.T. and Neuberg, S.L. (1990) 'A continuum of impression formation, from category-based to individuating processes: influences of information and motivation on attention and interpretation', in M.P. Zanna (ed.) *Advances in experimental social psychology*, vol. 23. London: Academic Press.

Fiske, S.T. and Taylor, S.E. (1991) *Social cognition*. 2nd edition. New York: McGraw-Hill.

Fiske, S.T., Neuberg, S.L., Beattie, A.E. and Milberg, S.J. (1987) 'Category-based and attribute-based reactions to others: some informational conditions of stereotyping and individuating processes', *Journal of Experimental Social Psychology*, 23, 399–427.

Fletcher, G.J.O. and Ward, C. (1988) 'Attribution theory and processes: a cross cultural perspective', in M.H. Bond (ed.) *The cross-cultural challenge to social psychology*. London: Sage.

Flew, A. (1975) *Thinking about thinking*. Glasgow: Collins.

Flick, U. (1998) 'Everyday knowledge in social psychology', in U. Flick (ed.) *The psychology of the social*. Cambridge: Cambridge University Press.

Fox, R. (1992a) 'Prejudice and the unfinished mind: a new look at an old failing', *Psychological Inquiry*, 3, 137–152.

Fox, R. (1992b) 'Prejudice and the unfinished task', *Psychological Inquiry*, 3, 194–198.

Gaertner, S.L., Dovidio, J.F., Anastasio, P.A., Bachman, B.A. and Rust, M.C. (1993) 'Reducing intergroup bias: the common ingroup identity model', *European Journal of Social Psychology*, 4, 1–26.

Gergen, K.J. (1985) 'The social constructionism movement in modern psychology', *American Psychologist*, 40, 266–275.

Gilbert, D.T. and Hixon, J.G. (1991) 'The trouble with thinking: activation and application of stereotypic beliefs', *Journal of Personality and Social Psychology*, 60, 509–517.

Gilbert, D.T., Pelham, B.W. and Krull, D.S. (1988) 'On cognitive busyness: when person perceivers meet person perceived', *Journal of Personality and Social Psychology*, 54, 733–739.

Gilbert, G.M. (1951) 'Stereotype persistence and change among college students', *Journal of Abnormal and Social Psychology*, 46, 245–254.

Gill, R. (1993) 'Justifying injustice: broadcasters' accounts of inequality in radio', in E. Burman and I. Parker (eds) *Discourse analytic research – repertoires and readings of texts in action*. London: Routledge.

Goffman, E. (1959) *The presentation of self in everyday life*. New York: Anchor Books.

Goldstone, R.L. and Barsalou, L.W. (1998) 'Reuniting perception and conception', *Cognition*, 65, 231–262.

Goren, C.C., Sarty, M. and Wu, R.W.K. (1975) 'Visual following and pattern discrimination of face-like stimuli by newborn infants', *Pediatrics*, 56, 544–549.

Hamilton, D.L. (1979) 'A cognitive-attributional analysis of stereotyping', in L. Berkowitz (ed.) *Advances in experimental social psychology*, vol. 12. New York: Academic Press.

Hamilton, D.L. and Gifford, R.K. (1976) 'Illusory correlation in interpersonal perception: a cognitive basis of stereotypic judgments', *Journal of Experimental Social Psychology*, 12, 392–407.

Hamilton, D.L. and Trolier, T.K. (1986) 'Stereotypes and stereotyping: an overview of the cognitive approach', in J.F. Dovidio and S.L. Gaertner (eds) *Prejudice, discrimination, and racism*. Orlando, Fla.: Academic Press.

Hamilton, D.L., Dugan, P.M. and Trolier, T.K. (1985) 'The formation of stereotypic beliefs: further evidence for distinctiveness-based illusory correlation', *Journal of Personality and Social Psychology*, 48, 5–17.

Harré, R. (1988) 'Accountability within a social order: the role of pronouns', in C. Antaki (ed.) *Analysing everyday explanation: a casebook of methods*. London: Sage.

Harré, R. (1998) 'The epistemology of social representations', in U. Flick (ed.) *The psychology of the social*. Cambridge: Cambridge University Press.

Harré, R. and Secord, P.F. (1972) *The explaation of social behaviour*. Oxford: Blackwell.

Hartley, E.L. (1946) *Problems in prejudice*. New York: King's Crown Press.

Haslam, S.A. and Turner, J.C. (1992) 'Context-dependent variation in social stereotyping 2: the relationship between frame of reference, self-categorization and accentuation', *European Journal of Social Psychology*, 22, 251–277.

Haslam, S.A., McGarty, C., and Brown, P.M. (1996) 'The search for differentiated meaning is a precursor to illusory correlation', *Personality and Social Psychology Bulletin*, 22, 611–619.

Hastie, R. (1981) 'Schematic principles in human memory', in E.T. Higgins, C.P. Herman and M.P. Zanna (eds) *Social cognition: the Ontario symposium*, vol. 1. Hillsdale, NJ: Erlbaum.

Hastie, R. and Kumar, P.A. (1979) 'Person memory: personality traits as organizing principles in memory for behaviours', *Journal of Personality and Social Psychology*, 37, 25–38.

Heider, F. (1958) *The psychology of interpersonal relations*. New York: Wiley.

Herzlich, C. (1973) *Health and illness: a social psychological analysis*. London: Academic Press.

Hewstone, M. (1997) 'Three lessons from social psychology: multiple levels of analysis, methodological pluralism, and statistical sophistication', in C. McGarty and S.A. Haslam (eds) *The message of social psychology*. Oxford: Blackwell.

Hewstone, M. and Augoustinos, M. (1998) 'Social attributions and social representations', in U. Flick (ed.) *The psychology of the social*. Cambridge: Cambridge University Press.

Hewstone, M. and Brown, R. (1986) 'Contact is not enough: an intergroup perspective on the "contact hypothesis"', In M. Hewstone and R. Brown (eds) *Contact and conflict in intergroup encounters*. Oxford: Blackwell.

Hewstone, M., Jaspers, J.M.F. and Lalljee, M. (1982) 'Social representations, social attribution and social identity. The intergroup images of "Public" and "Comprehensive" schoolboys', *European Journal of Social Psychology*, 12, 241–269.

Hewstone, M., Hopkins, N. and Routh, D. (1992) 'Cognitive models of stereotype change: I. Generalization and subtyping in young people's views of the police', *European Journal of Social Psychology*, 22, 219–234.

Hewstone, M., Macrae, C.N., Griffiths, R. and Milne, A.B. (1994) 'Cognitive models of stereotype change: 5. Measurement, development, and consequences of subtyping', *Journal of Experimental Social Psychology*, 30, 505–526.

Hinkle, S. and Brown, R.J. (1990) 'Social identity theory processes: some limitations and limiting conditions', in D. Abrams and M.A. Hogg (eds) *Social identity theory: constructive and critical advances.* Hemel Hempstead: Harvester Wheatsheaf.

Hinton, P.R. (1993) *The psychology of interpersonal perception.* London: Routledge.

Hoffman, C. and Hurst, N. (1990) 'Gender stereotypes: perception or rationalization?', *Journal of Personality and Social Psychology*, 58, 197–208.

Hofstede, G. (1980) *Culture's consequences: international differences in work-related values.* Beverly Hills, Calif.: Sage.

Holdaway, S. (1999) 'Understanding the police investigation of the murder of Stephen Lawrence: A "mundane sociological analysis"', *Sociological Research Online*, 4, 1. http://www.socresonline.org.uk/socresonline/4/1/holdaway.html

Ito, T.A., Larsen, J.T., Smith, N.K. and Cacioppo, J.T. (1998) 'Negative information weighs more heavily on the brain: the negativity bias in evaluative categorizations', *Journal of Personality and Social Psychology*, 75, 887–900.

Jackson, L.A. and Ervin, K.S. (1992) 'Height stereotypes of women and men: the liability of shortness for both sexes', *Journal of Social Psychology*, 132, 433–445.

James, W. (1890) *The principles of psychology.* Volume 2. New York: Dover (Dover edition 1950).

Jodelet, D. (1991) *Madness and social representations.* Hemel Hempstead: Harvester Wheatsheaf.

Johnson, L. (1996) 'Resisting change: information-seeking and stereotype change', *European Journal of Social Psychology*, 26, 799–825.

Johnson, L. and Hewstone, M. (1992) 'Cognitive models of stereotype change: III. Subtyping and the perceived typicality of disconfirming group members', *Journal of Experimental Social Psychology*, 28, 360–386.

Johnson-Laird, P.N. (1983) *Mental models*. Cambridge: Cambridge University Press.

Jones, E.E. and Davis, K.E. (1965) 'From acts to dispositions: the attributional process in person perception', in L. Berkowitz (ed.) *Advances in experimental social psychology*, 2. New York: Academic Press.

Jones, E.E. and McGillis, D. (1976) 'Correspondent inferences and the attribution cube: a comparative reappraisal', in J.H. Harvey, W.J. Ickes and R.F. Kidd (eds) *New directions in attribution research*, vol. 1. Hillsdale, NJ: Erlbaum.

Jones, E.E. and Nisbett, R.E. (1971) 'The actor and the observer: divergent perceptions of the causes of behaviour', in E.E. Jones, D.E. Kanouse, H.H. Kelley, R.E. Nisbett, S. Valins and B. Weiner (eds) *Attribution: perceiving the causes of behaviour*. Morristown, NJ: General Learning Press.

Jones, M. (1997) 'Preventing the application of stereotypic biases in the courtroom: the role of detailed testimony', *Journal of Applied Social Psychology*, 27, 1767–1784.

Judd, C.M. and Park, B. (1993) 'Definition and assessment of accuracy in social stereotypes', *Psychological Review*, 100, 109–128.

Jussim, L., Coleman, L.M. and Lerch, L. (1987) 'The nature of stereotypes: a comparison and integration of three theories', *Journal of Personality and Social Psychology*, 52, 536–546.

Jussim, L., Eccles, J. and Madon, S. (1996) 'Social perception, social stereotypes, and teacher perceptions: accuracy and the search for the powerful self-fulfilling prophesy', in M.P. Zanna (ed.) *Advances in experimental social psychology*, vol. 28. New York: Academic Press.

Kahneman, D. (1973) *Attention and effort*. Englewood Cliffs, NJ: Prentice Hall.

Kahneman, D. and Tversky, A. (1973) 'On the psychology of prediction', *Psychological Review*, 80, 237–251.

Kahneman, D., Slovic, P. and Tversky, A. (1982) *Judgement under uncertainty: heuristics and biases*. Cambridge: Cambridge University Press.

Karlins, M., Coffman, T.L. and Walters, G. (1969) 'On the fading of social stereotypes: studies in three generations of college students', *Journal of Personality and Social Psychology*, 13, 1–16.

Katz, D. and Braly, K.W. (1933) 'Racial prejudice and racial stereotypes', *Journal of Abnormal and Social Psychology*, 30, 175–193.

Katz, E., Liebes, T. and Iwao, S. (1991) 'Neither here nor there: why "Dallas" failed in Japan', *Communication*, 12, 99–110.

Kelley, H.H. (1967) 'Attribution theory in social psychology', *Nebraska Symposium on Motivation*, 15, 192–238.

Kelley, H.H. (1973) 'The process of casual attribution', *American Psychologist*, 28, 107–128.

Kelly, G.A. (1955) *A theory of personality: the theory of personal constructs*. New York: Norton.

Kerr, N.L. (1978) 'Beautiful and blameless: effects of victim attractiveness and responsibility on the judgements of mock jurors', *Personality and Social Psychology Bulletin*, 4, 479–482.

Kunda, Z. and Oleson, K.C. (1995) 'Maintaining stereotypes in the face of disconfirmation: constructing grounds for subtyping deviants', *Journal of Personality and Social Psychology*, 68, 565–579.

Kunda, Z. and Oleson, K.C. (1997) 'When exceptions prove the rule: how the extremity of deviance determines the impact of deviant examples on stereotypes', *Journal of Personality and Social Psychology*, 72, 965–979.

Kunda, Z., Sinclair, L. and Griffin, D. (1997) 'Equal ratings but separate meanings: stereotypes and the construal of traits', *Journal of Personality and Social Psychology*, 72, 720–734.

Lakoff, G. (1987) *Women, fire and dangerous things. What categories reveal about the mind*. Chicago: University of Chicago Press (paperback edition 1990).

Lalonde, R.N. and Gardner, R.C. (1989) 'An intergroup perspective on stereotype organization and processing', *British Journal of Social Psychology*, 28, 289–303.

Landy, D. and Sigall, H. (1974) 'Beauty is talent: task evaluation as a function of the performer's physical attractiveness', *Journal of Personality and Social Psychology*, 29, 299–304.

Langer, E.J. (1978) 'Rethinking the role of thought in social interaction', in J.H. Harvey, W. Ickes and R.F. Kidd (eds) *New directions in attribution research*, vol. 2. Hilldale, NJ: Erlbaum.

191

Lepore, L. and Brown, R. (1997) 'Category and stereotype activation: is prejudice inevitable?', *Journal of Personality and Social Psychology*, 72, 275–287.

Lerner, M. (1980) *The belief in a just world: a fundamental delusion*. New York: Plenum.

Lerner, M. and Miller, D. (1978) 'Just world research and the attribution process: looking back and ahead', *Psychological Bulletin*, 85, 1030–1051.

Lewis, M. (1992) 'Many minds make madness: judgment under uncertainty and certainty', *Psychological Inquiry*, 3, 170–172.

Liebes, T. and Katz, E. (1986) 'Patterns of involvement in television fiction: a comparative analysis', *European Journal of Communication*, 1, 151–171.

Linville, P.W. and Jones, E.E. (1980) 'Polarized appraisal of out-group members', *Journal of Personality and Social Psychology*, 38, 689–703.

Lippmann, W. (1922) *Public opinion*. New York: Macmillan.

Lombroso, C. and Ferrero, G. (1896) *La Femme criminelle et la prostituée*. Paris: Germer Bailliere.

McArthur, L.Z. (1972) 'The how and what of why: some determinants and consequences of causal attribution', *Journal of Personality and Social Psychology*, 22, 171–193.

McGarty, C. and Penny, R.E.C. (1988) 'Categorization, accentuation and social judgement', *British Journal of Social Psychology*, 27, 147–157.

MacPherson, W., Sir (1999) *The Stephen Lawrence inquiry*. URL http://www.official-documents.co.uk/document/cm42/4262/4262.htm.

Macrae, C.N. and Shepherd, J.W. (1989) 'Do criminal stereotypes mediate juridic judgements?', *British Journal of Social Psychology*, 28, 189–191.

Macrae, C.N., Hewstone, M. and Griffiths, R.J. (1993) 'Processing load and memory for stereotype-based information', *European Journal of Social Psychology*, 23, 77–87.

Macrae, C.N., Milne, A.B. and Bodenhausen, G.V. (1994) 'Stereotypes as energy-saving devices: a peek inside the cognitive toolbox', *Journal of Personality and Social Psychology*, 66, 37–47.

Mayer, J.D. and Bower, G.H. (1986) 'Learning and memory for personality prototypes', *Journal of Personality and Social Psychology*, 51, 473–492.

Mervis, C.B. and Rosch, E. (1981) 'Categorization of natural objects', *Annual Review of Psychology*, 32, 89–115.

Miller, D.T. and Ross, M. (1975) 'Self-serving biases in the attribution of causality: fact or fiction?', *Psychological Bulletin*, 82, 213–225.

Mischel, W. (1968) *Personality and assessment*. New York: Wiley.

Mischel, W. (1973) 'Towards a cognitive social learning reconceptualization of personality', *Psychological Review*, 80, 252–283.

Morales, J.F., López-Sáez, M. and Vega, L. (1998) 'Discrimination and beliefs on discrimination in individualists and collectivists', in S. Worchel, J.P. Morales, D. Páez and J.-C. Deschamps (eds) *Social identity: international perspectives*. London: Sage.

Moray, N. (1959) 'Attention in dichotic listening: affective cues and the influence of instructions', *Quarterly Journal of Experimental Psychology*, 11, 56–60.

Moscovici, S. (1961) *La Psychoanalyse: son image et son public*. Paris: Presses Universitaires de France.

Moscovici, S. (1973) 'Foreword', in C. Herzlich, *Health and illness: a social psychological analysis*. London: Academic Press.

Moscovici, S. (1984) 'The phenomenon of social representations', in R.M. Farr and S. Moscovici (eds) *Social representations*. Cambridge: Cambridge University Press.

Moscovici, S. (1997) *Social representations theory and social constructionism*. URL http://www.nsu.ru/psych/internet/bits/mosc1.htm.

Moscovici, S. (1998) 'The history and actuality of social representations', in U. Flick (ed.) *The psychology of the social*. Cambridge: Cambridge University Press.

Moscovici, S. and Hewstone, M. (1983) 'Social representations and social explanation: from the "naïve" to the "amateur" scientist', in M. Hewstone (ed.) *Attribution theory: social and functional extensions*. Oxford: Blackwell.

Mullen, B., Brown, R.J. and Smith, C. (1992) 'Ingroup bias as a function of salience, relevance and status: an integration', *European Journal of Social Psychology*, 22, 103–112.

Mummendey, A. and Schreiber, H.-J. (1983) 'Better or just different? Positive social identity by discrimination against, or by differentiation from outgroups', *European Journal of Social Psychology*, 13, 389–397.

Mummendey, A. and Schreiber, H.-J. (1984) 'Different just means better: some obvious and some hidden pathways to ingroup favouritism', *British Journal of Social Psychology*, 23, 363–368.

Nelson, T.E., Acker, M. and Manis, M. (1996) 'Irrepressible stereotypes', *Journal of Experimental Social Psychology*, 32, 13–38.

Neuberg, S.L. (1992) 'Evolution and individuation: the adaptiveness of nonstereotypical thought', *Psychological Inquiry*, 3, 178–180.

Oakes, P.J. and Reynolds, K.J. (1997) 'Asking the accuracy question: is measurement the answer?', in R. Spears, P.J. Oakes, N. Ellemers and S.A. Haslam (eds) *The social psychology of stereotyping and group life*. Oxford: Blackwell.

Oakes, P.J., Turner, J.C. and Haslam, S.A. (1991) 'Perceiving people as group members: the role of fit in the salience of social categories', *British Journal of Social Psychology*, 30, 125–144.

Oakes, P.J., Haslam, S.A. and Turner, J.C. (1997) 'The role of proto-typicality in group influence and cohesion: contextual variation in the graded structure of social categories', In R. Spears, P.J. Oakes, N. Ellemers and S.A. Haslam (eds) *The social psychology of stereo-typing and group life*. Oxford: Blackwell.

Oyserman, D. and Markus, H.R. (1998) 'Self as social representation', in U. Flick (ed.) *The psychology of the social*. Cambridge: Cambridge University Press.

Pan, B.A. and Gleason, J. Berko (1997) 'Semantic development: learning the meaning of words', in J. Berko Gleason (ed.) *The development of language*. 4th edition. Boston, Mass.: Allyn & Bacon.

Pavelchak, M.A. (1989) 'Piecemeal and category-based evaluation: an ideographic analysis', *Journal of Personality and Social Psychology*, 56, 354–363.

Pendry, L. (1998) 'When the mind is otherwise engaged: resource depletion and social stereotyping', *European Journal of Social Psychology*, 28, 293–299.

Petty, R.E. and Cacioppo, J.T. (1985) 'The elaboration likelihood model of persuasion', in L. Berkowitz (ed.) *Advances in experimental social psychology*, vol. 19. New York: Academic Press.

Porter, D. (ed.) (1997) *Internet culture*. London: Routledge.

Posner, M.I. and Snyder, C.R.R. (1975) 'Attention and cognitive control', in R.L. Solso (ed.) *Information processing and cognition: the Loyola symposium*. Hillsdale, NJ: Erlbaum.

Potter, J. (1996) 'Attitudes, social representations and discursive psychology', in M. Wetherell (ed.) *Identities, groups and social issues*. London: Sage.

Potter, J. and Wetherell, M. (1987) *Discourse and social psychology: beyond attitudes and behaviour*. London: Sage.

Potter, J. and Wetherell, M. (1998) 'Social representations, discourse analysis, and racism', in U. Flick (ed.) *The psychology of the social*. Cambridge: Cambridge University Press.

Pratto, F. and Bargh, J.A. (1991) 'Stereotyping based on apparently individuating information: trait and global components of sex stereotypes under attention overload', *Journal of Experimental Social Psychology*, 27, 26–47.

Reicher, S., Hopkins, N. and Condor, S. (1997) 'Stereotype construction as a strategy of influence', in R. Spears, P.J. Oakes, N. Ellemers and S.A. Haslam (eds) *The social psychology of stereotyping and group life*. Oxford: Blackwell.

Reiss, M., Rosenfeld, P., Melburg, V. and Tedeschi, J.T. (1981) 'Self-serving attributions: biased private perceptions and distorted public perceptions', *Journal of Personality and Social Psychology*, 41, 224–251.

Robertson, S.I. (1999) *Types of thinking*. London: Routledge.

Roese, N.J. and Olson, J.M. (1996) 'Counterfactuals, causal attributions, and the hindsight bias: a conceptual integration', *Journal of Experimental Social Psychology*, 32, 197–227.

Rosch, E. (1973) 'On the internal structure of perceptual and semantic categories', in T.E. Moore (ed.) *Cognitive development and the acquisition of language*. London: Academic Press.

Rosch, E. (1975) 'Cognitive representations of semantic categories', *Journal of Experimental Psychology: General*, 104, 3, 192–233.

Rosch, E. (1978) 'Principles of categorization', in E. Rosch and B.B. Lloyd (eds) *Cognition and categorization*. Hillsdale, NJ: Erlbaum.

Rosch, E. and Mervis, C.B. (1975) 'Family resemblances: studies in the internal structure of categories', *Cognitive Psychology*, 7, 573–605.

Rosch, E., Mervis, C., Gray, W., Johnson, D. and Boyes-Braem, P. (1976) 'Basic objects in natural categories', *Cognitive Psychology*, 382–439.

Rosenberg, S. and Jones, R.A. (1972) 'A method for investigating and representing a person's implicit personality theory: Theodore Dreiser's view of people', *Journal of Personality and Social Psychology*, 22, 373–386.

Ross, L. (1977) 'The intuitive psychologist and his shortcomings: distortions in the attribution process', in L. Berkowitz (ed.) *Advances in experimental social psychology*, vol. 10. New York: Academic Press.

Ross, L., Greene, D. and House, P. (1977) 'The 'false consensus effect': an egocentric bias in social perception and attribution processes', *Journal of Experimental Social Psychology*, 13, 279–301.

Roth, I. (1986) 'Conceptual categories', in I. Roth and J.P. Frisby, *Perception and representation: a cognitive approach*. Milton Keynes: Open University Press.

Ryckman, R.M., Robbins, M.A., Kaczor, L.M. and Gold, J.A. (1989) 'Male and female raters' stereotyping of male and female physiques', *Personality and Social Psychology Bulletin*, 15, 244–251.

Sacks, O. (1985) *The man who mistook his wife for a hat*. London: Duckworth (Picador edition, 1986, London: Pan Books).

Schank, R.C. and Abelson, R.P. (1977) *Scripts, plans, goals and understanding*. Hillsdale, NJ: Erlbaum.

Schneider, W. and Shiffrin, R.M. (1977) 'Controlled and automatic human information processing: I. detection, search, and attention', *Psychological Review*, 84, 1–66.

Scribner, S. (1977) 'Models of thinking and ways of speaking: culture and logic reconsidered', in P.N. Johnson-Laird and P.C. Wason (eds) *Thinking: readings in cognitive science*. Cambridge: Cambridge University Press.

Secord, P.F. and Backman, C.W. (1974) *Social psychology*. 2nd edition. Tokyo: McGraw-Hill.

Semin, G.R. (1980) 'A gloss on attribution theory', *British Journal of Social and Clinical Psychology*, 19, 291–300.

Semin, G.R. and Manstead, A.S.R. (1983) *Accountability of conduct*. London: Academic Press.

Shaver, K.G. (1970) 'Defensive attribution: effects of severity and relevance on the responsibility assigned for an accident', *Journal of Personality and Social Psychology*, 14, 101–113.

Sheldon, W.H. (1942) *The varieties of temperament: a psychology of constitutional differences*. New York: Harper.

Sherif, M. (1966) *In common predicament: social psychology of intergroup conflict and cooperation*. Boston, Mass.: Houghton Mifflin.

Sherif, M., Harvey, O.J., White, B.J., Hood, W.E. and Sherif, C.W. (1961) *Intergroup conflict and cooperation: the robber's cave experiment*. Norman, Okla.: University of Oklahoma Book Exchange.

Sherman, J.W. (1996) 'Development and mental representation of stereotypes', *Journal of Personality and Social Psychology*, 70, 1126–1141.

Sherman, J.W., Lee, A.Y., Bessenoff, G.R. and Frost, L.A. (1998) 'Stereotype efficiency reconsidered: encoding flexibility under cognitive load', *Journal of Personality and Social Psychology*, 75, 589–606.

Shiffrin, R.M. and Schneider, W. (1977) 'Controlled and automatic human information processing: II. perceptual learning, automatic attending and a general theory', *Psychological Review*, 84, 127–190.

Sigall, H. and Ostrove, N. (1975) 'Beautiful but dangerous: effects of offender attractiveness and nature of the crime on juridic judgements', *Journal of Personality and Social Psychology*, 31, 410–414.

Skowronski, J.J. and Carlson, S.E. (1989) 'Negativity and extremity biases in impression formation: a review of explanations', *Psychological Bulletin*, 105, 131–142.

Smith, A.E., Jussim, L., Eccles, J., VanNoy, M., Madon, S. and Palumbo, P. (1998) 'Self-fulfilling prophesies, perceptual biases, and accuracy at the individual and group levels', *Journal of Experimental Social Psychology*, 34, 530–561.

Smith, E.R. and Zárate, M.A. (1992) 'Exemplar-based model of social judgment', *Psychological Review*, 99, 3–21.

Smith, P.E. and Bond, M.H. (1998) *Social psychology across cultures*. 2nd edition. Hemel Hempstead: Prentice Hall Europe.

Snyder, M., Tanke, E.D. and Berscheid, E. (1977) 'Social perception and interpersonal behaviour: on the self-fulfilling nature of social stereotypes', *Journal of Personality and Social Psychology*, 35, 656–666.

Snyder, M., Campbell, B.H. and Preston, E. (1982) 'Testing hypotheses about human nature: assessing the accuracy of social stereotypes', *Social Cognition*, 1, 256–272.

Sommer, C.M. (1998) 'Social representations and media communications', in U. Flick (ed.) *The psychology of the social*. Cambridge: Cambridge University Press.

Spears, R. and Manstead, A.S.R. (1989) 'The social context of stereotyping and differentiation', *European Journal of Social Psychology*, 19, 101–121.

Stangor, C. and Lange, J.E. (1994) 'Mental representations of social groups: advances in understanding stereotypes and stereotyping', in M.P. Zanna (ed.) *Advances in Experimental Social Psychology*, 26, 357–416.

Stapel, D.A. and Koomen, W. (1998) 'When stereotype activation results in (counter)stereotypical judgements: priming stereotype-relevant traits and exemplars', *Journal of Experimental Social Psychology*, 34, 136–163.

Stewart, R.A., Powell, G.E. and Chetwynd, S.J. (1979) *Person perception and stereotyping*. Westmead: Saxon House.

Tajfel, H. (1969) 'Cognitive aspects of prejudice', *Journal of Social Issues*, 25, 4, 79–93.

Tajfel, H. (1970) 'Experiments in intergroup discrimination', *Scientific American*, 223, 5, 96–102.

Tajfel, H. (1978a) 'Intergroup behaviour: I. individualistic perspectives', in H. Tajfel and C. Fraser (eds) *Introducing social psychology*. Harmondsworth: Penguin.

Tajfel, H. (1978b) 'Intergroup behaviour: II. group perspectives', in H. Tajfel and C. Fraser (eds) *Introducing social psychology*. Harmondsworth: Penguin.

Tajfel, H. (1978c) *Differentiation between social groups: studies in the social psychology of intergroup relations*. London: Academic Press.

Tajfel, H. and Turner, J.C. (1979) 'An integrative theory of intergroup conflict', in W.G. Austin and S. Worchel (eds) *The social psychology of intergroup relations*. Monterey, Calif.: Brooks/Cole.

Tajfel, H. and Wilkes, A.L. (1963) 'Classification and quantitative judgement', *British Journal of Social and Clinical Psychology*, 54, 101–114.

Tajfel, H., Flament, C., Billig, M., and Bundy, R. (1971) 'Social categorization and intergroup behaviour', *European Journal of Social Psychology*, 1, 149–178.

Taylor, D.M. and Porter, L.E. (1994) 'A multicultural view of stereotyping', in W.J. Lonner and R.S. Malpass (eds) *Psychology and culture*. Boston, Mass.: Allyn & Bacon.

Taylor, S.E., Fiske, S.T., Etcoff, N.L. and Ruderman, A.J. (1978) 'Categorical and contextual bases of person memory and stereotyping', *Journal of Personality and Social Psychology*, 38, 7, 778–793.

Thorndike, E.L. (1920) 'A constant error in psychological ratings', *Journal of Applied Psychology*, 4, 25–29.

Treisman, A.M. (1964) 'Verbal cues, language, and meaning in selective attention', *American Journal of Psychology*, 77, 206–219.

Treisman, A.M. (1988) 'Features and objects: the 14th Bartlett memorial lecture', *Quarterly Journal of Experimental Psychology*, 40A, 201–237.

Turner, J.C. (1975) 'Social comparison and social identity: some prospects for intergroup behaviour', *European Journal of Social Psychology*, 5, 1–31.

Turner, J.C. (1987) 'A self-categorization theory', in J.C. Turner, M.A. Hogg, P.J. Oakes, S.D. Reicher and M.S. Wetherell, *Rediscovering the social group: a self-categorization theory*. Oxford: Blackwell.

Turner, J.C. (1991) *Social influence*. Milton Keynes: Open University Press.

Tversky, A. and Kahneman, D. (1973) 'Availability: a heuristic for judging frequency and probability', *Cognitive Psychology*, 4, 207–232.

Tversky, A. and Kahneman, D. (1982) 'Judgments of and by representativeness', in D. Kahneman, P. Slovic and A. Tversky (eds) *Judgement under uncertainty: heuristics and biases*. Cambridge: Cambridge University Press.

van Knippenberg, A. (1984) 'Intergroup differences in group perceptions', in H. Tajfel (ed.) *The social dimension: European developments in social psychology*. Cambridge: Cambridge University Press.

van Knippenberg, A. and Dijksterhuis, A. (1996) 'A posteriori stereotype activation: the preservation of stereotypes through memory distortion', *Social Cognition*, 14, 21–53.

van Langenhove, L. and Harré, R. (1994) 'Cultural stereotypes and positioning theory', *Journal for the Theory of Social Behaviour*, 24, 359–372.

Wason, P.C. (1966) 'Reasoning', in B.M. Foss (ed.) *New horizons in psychology*. Harmondsworth: Penguin.

Weber, R. and Crocker, J. (1983) 'Cognitive processes in the revision of stereotypic beliefs', *Journal of Personality and Social Psychology*, 45, 961–977.

Welford, A.T. (1967) *Fundamentals of skill*. London: Methuen.

Wetherell, M. and Potter, J. (1988) 'Discourse analysis and the identification of interpretive repertoires', in C. Antaki (ed.) *Analysing everyday explanation: a casebook of methods*. London: Sage.

Wittenbrink, B., Judd, C.M. and Park, B. (1997) 'Evidence for racial prejudice at the implicit level and its relationship with questionnaire measures', *Journal of Personality and Social Psychology*, 72, 262–274.

Wolff, P.H. (1966) 'The natural history of crying and other vocalizations in early infancy', in B.M. Foss (ed.) *Determinants of infant behaviour*, vol. 4. London: Methuen.

Woodworth, R.S. and Sells, S.B. (1935) 'An atmosphere effect in formal syllogistic reasoning', *Journal of Experimental Psychology*, 18, 451–460.

Worchel, S. and Rothgerber, H. (1997) 'Changing the stereotype of the stereotype', in R. Spears, P.J. Oakes, N. Ellemers and S.A. Haslam (eds) *The social psychology of stereotyping and group life*. Oxford: Blackwell.

Yzerbyt, V., Rocher, S. and Schadron, G. (1997) 'Stereotypes as explanations: a subjective essentialistic view of group perception', in R. Spears, P.J. Oakes, N. Ellemers and S.A. Haslam (eds) *The social psychology of stereotyping and group life*. Oxford: Blackwell.

Index

INDEX